D1740415

ALICE IN
WATERLAND

ALICE IN WATERLAND

~

Lewis Carroll and the River Thames in Oxford

MARK DAVIES

Oxford Towpath Press

First published in the UK in
2010 by Signal Books, Oxford

Second edition 2012.
This cloth edition published 2023.

Oxford Towpath Press

Thanks are due to the trustees of the Greening Lamborn Trust,
whose objective is to promote public interest in the history, architecture,
old photographs, and heritage of Oxford and its neighbourhood by
supporting publications of other media that create access to them.

A catalogue record for this book is available from the British Library.

ISBN 978-0-9535593-8-1 Cloth

Designed by Bryony Clark

Printed & bound in Great Britain by
TJ Books Limited, Padstow, Cornwall

CONTENTS

MAPS & ILLUSTRATIONS

MAPS

ILLUSTRATIONS

FOREWORD TO THE FIRST AND SECOND EDITIONS

Many people are unaware that *Alice's Adventures in Wonderland* was inspired by a river trip that included the author, his friend, and three young children. Lorina, Alice, and Edith Liddell encouraged the telling of the tale, but it was Alice who asked Lewis Carroll to write down the story, thus preserving a spontaneous adventure that could so easily have been lost to memory.

This merry crew appear in the story from time to time, sometimes moderately disguised, and there are many references to Oxford – its events and personalities.

Alice in Waterland is the only book I am aware of that focuses on the rivers of Oxford that provide the background to the famous river-trip and other excursions with the Liddells. Mark Davies quotes both *Alice* books for all appropriate river references, and adds extracts from Lewis Carroll's private diaries to set the scene. Profusely illustrated with maps, photographs, and other images of the day, his book brings the locations of the story vividly to life.

The book includes much background information drawn from other contemporary writers to help us empathise with the Victorian times and events. Thorough research provides much that is not found elsewhere in Carroll biographies, and corrects a few long-standing errors about the people and places involved in the making of this most famous of children's stories.

EDWARD WAKELING
editor of *Lewis Carroll's Diaries*, 2010

PREFACE

'There ought to be a book written about me, that there ought!' says Alice in *Alice's Adventures in Wonderland*. And there was, of course: first the fantasy from which Alice's statement comes, then a sequel, and countless books of analysis, reminiscence, comment, and translation ever since.

Strangely, none of the writers of these books had ever analysed this world-famous subject in a world-famous city specifically from the crucial and obvious perspective of the River Thames until the publication of the first edition of *Alice in Waterland* in 2010. Yet the influence of the river in the creation of *Wonderland* and *Through the Looking-Glass* is enormous. Indeed, had there been no river, there would have been no 'Alice'. The river provided the opportunities to invent many of the tales, created the conditions for the decision to write them down, and inspired many of the two books' episodes.

It is the latter point which is of greatest interest to me, as an Oxford local historian and occupant of a residential narrowboat – 'Bill the Lizard', as it happens – for nearly thirty years. Charles Dodgson's supposed and actual incorporation of real places, people, and incidents has produced many theories over the years, some of them bizarre enough to have been worthy of Wonderland itself. It has been pleasing to provide, from the perspective of the riverbank, confirmatory, additional, or new information relating to some of these ideas. It has also been gratifying, and a little surprising, to learn so much about Victorian Oxford through characters such as the Hatter, the Sheep, and the Red Queen! The current edition has been much revised, but retains broadly the same format, albeit the previous editions' appendices on 'Trill Mill Stream' and 'The Oxford–Cambridge Boat Race of 1843' have been replaced with more pertinent accounts of 'Alice's Shop' and 'The Diaries of Thomas Vere Bayne'.

In terms of conventions, Charles Dodgson's pen-name of Lewis Carroll (first adopted in 1856) has been used throughout the main text, but not in the 'Important Dates' section, where his real life deserved, I felt, his real name. The day of the week has been included in the extracts from Charles Dodgson's diaries only when deemed important to the context of the comment. I have usually relied on the uncanny accuracy of Edward Wakeling's years of birth and death for the individuals mentioned either in passing or, often, taken from his transcription of Lewis Carroll's *Diaries*. Meticulously indexed, with extraordinarily detailed biographical and contextual notes, these ten volumes published by the Lewis Carroll Society (preceded in the 1950s by Roger Lancelyn Green's abridged transcriptions) are the principal source of practically every piece of Lewis Carroll/Alice analysis that has ever been published, and the means by which the enigmatic genius of Lewis Carroll eludes the privileged and confined clutches of academics and historians to become accessible to us all.

The images have been selected to try to convey the river scene as it would have appeared to Dodgson and the Liddell girls from the 1850s to the 1870s. With one exception, the earliest is from 1848 (three years before Carroll's arrival in Oxford); the latest (apart from my own) is dated 1900 (two years after his death). Some of the excerpts from novels and memoirs are not precisely contemporaneous with the direct experience of the protagonists, but nonetheless help to portray and explain a river whose appearance and nature tend in any case to change but slowly. I am pleased to note that Dr William Sanday thought that a watery theme was apt in the tribute he preached at Christ Church on the Sunday after Dodgson's death in 1898: 'may we not say that from our courts at Christ Church there has flowed into the literature of our time a rill, bright and sparkling, health-giving and purifying, wherever its waters extended?'.

1500 copies were printed of the first edition of this book and 2000 of the second. My thanks for assistance in producing all three editions go (in more or less chronological order) to Luke Gander; my brother Nic ap Glyn for early feedback; Judith Curthoys, Christ Church archivist; Mark

Richards and Edward Wakeling of the Lewis Carroll Society; Sir Philip Pullman (also for his crucial role in the ongoing campaign to preserve a boatyard facility in Jericho); Catherine Robinson and Bryony Clark, editor and designer respectively; James Ferguson of Signal Books; Stephanie Jenkins, whose www.headington.org website has been an invaluable research tool; Tim Metcalfe, formerly of the Oxford Times; Karl Wallendszus for the photograph of the Liddell Door; Tim Cox at Oxford Town Hall and David Pennant for the photographs of Thomas Randall; John Stainer & Andrew Stainer for the extracts from the unpublished diaries of Thomas Randall, and David & Genefer Clark for those of Richard James Spiers; Valerie Petts for the cover illustrations and Adrian Arbib for photographing them; Frideswide Curry for the photograph of Theophilus Carter; Christina Neagu at Christ Church Library; Selwyn Goodacre in respect of 'Alice's Shop'; and Jessica Woodward at Pusey House Library. In addition I would like to acknowledge the ever-helpful staff at Oxford's Bodleian Library and Oxfordshire History Centre.

Enough! You are no doubt anxious to join the 'merry party' on the river, to 'begin at the beginning ... and go on till you come to the end. Then stop.' All aboard then …

MARK JOHNSTONE DAVIES
Oxford, November 2022

SOME IMPORTANT DATES

27 Jan. 1832	Charles Lutwidge Dodgson (1832–1898) born Daresbury, Cheshire.
	His parents, Rev. Charles (1800–1868) and Frances Jane (née Lutwidge) Dodgson (1803–1851), already had two daughters: Frances/'Fanny' (1828–1903) and Elizabeth (1830–1916).
	Subsequent children were: Caroline (1833–1904), Mary (1835–1911), Skeffington (1836–1919), Wilfred (1838–1914), Louise (1840–1930), Margaret (1841–1915), Henrietta (1843–1922), and Edwin (1846–1918).
Early 1843	Family moved to Croft, Yorkshire. Dodgson attended Richmond Grammar School 1844 to 1846 and Rugby 1846 to 1849.
24 Jan. 1851	Dodgson commenced studies at Christ Church, just two days before the death of his mother. He graduated with a third-class degree in classics and a first in mathematics at the end of 1854.
4 May 1852	Alice Pleasance Liddell (1852–1934) born in London, as too her siblings Edward Henry i.e. Harry (1847–1911), Lorina Charlotte (1849–1930), and Edith Mary (1854–1876). Rhoda Caroline Anne (1859–1949) and Violet Constance (1864–1927) were born in Oxford, plus two further boys, Frederick Francis (1865–1950) and Lionel Charles (1868–1942).
14 Feb. 1855	Dodgson appointed sub-librarian at Christ Church, in place of his lifelong friend Thomas Vere Bayne.
30 June 1855	Alice's father, Henry George Liddell (1811–1898), installed as Dean of Christ Church.
25 Feb. 1856	Dodgson's first diary reference to the Liddell children.
1 Mar. 1856	'Lewis Carroll' used as Charles Dodgson's pen-name, when writing for *The Train*.

25 April 1856	Dodgson's first introduction to Alice.
3 June 1856	First known boat trip with Harry Liddell.
5 June 1856	First known boat trip with Ina (Lorina) Liddell.

[Diaries for April 1858 – May 1862 missing.]

22 Dec. 1861	Dodgson ordained as a deacon by the Bishop of Oxford.
26 May 1862	First known boat trip with Alice Liddell.
4 July 1862	The boat trip to Godstow, acknowledged as the day the story was created. Dodgson began writing in earnest on 13 November 1862, finished on 10 February 1863, and presented the handwritten manuscript of 'Alice's Adventures under Ground' to Alice on 26 November 1864.
25 June 1863	Last boat trip with the Liddell sisters.
14 May 1865	Dodgson preached his first Oxford sermon, at St Paul's, Jericho.
4 July 1865	*Alice's Adventures in Wonderland* printed in Oxford, then withdrawn, and reprinted in London later that year.
21 June 1868	Death of Dodgson's father, followed by relocation of his sisters and Aunt Lucy Lutwidge to Guildford.
6 Dec. 1871	First copy of *Through the Looking-Glass* received by Dodgson, although published as '1872'. Further editions were in 1878, 1887, and 1897 (the same year that edition nine of *Wonderland* was published).
15 Sept. 1880	Alice Liddell married Reginald Hargreaves (1852–1926) and moved to Lyndhurst, Hampshire.
22 Dec. 1886	*Alice's Adventures under Ground*, Dodgson's handwritten original four chapters, published in facsimile.
25 Mar. 1890	*The Nursery Alice* published.
14 Jan. 1898	Death of Charles Dodgson at Guildford.
16 Nov. 1934	Death of Alice Hargreaves (née Liddell).

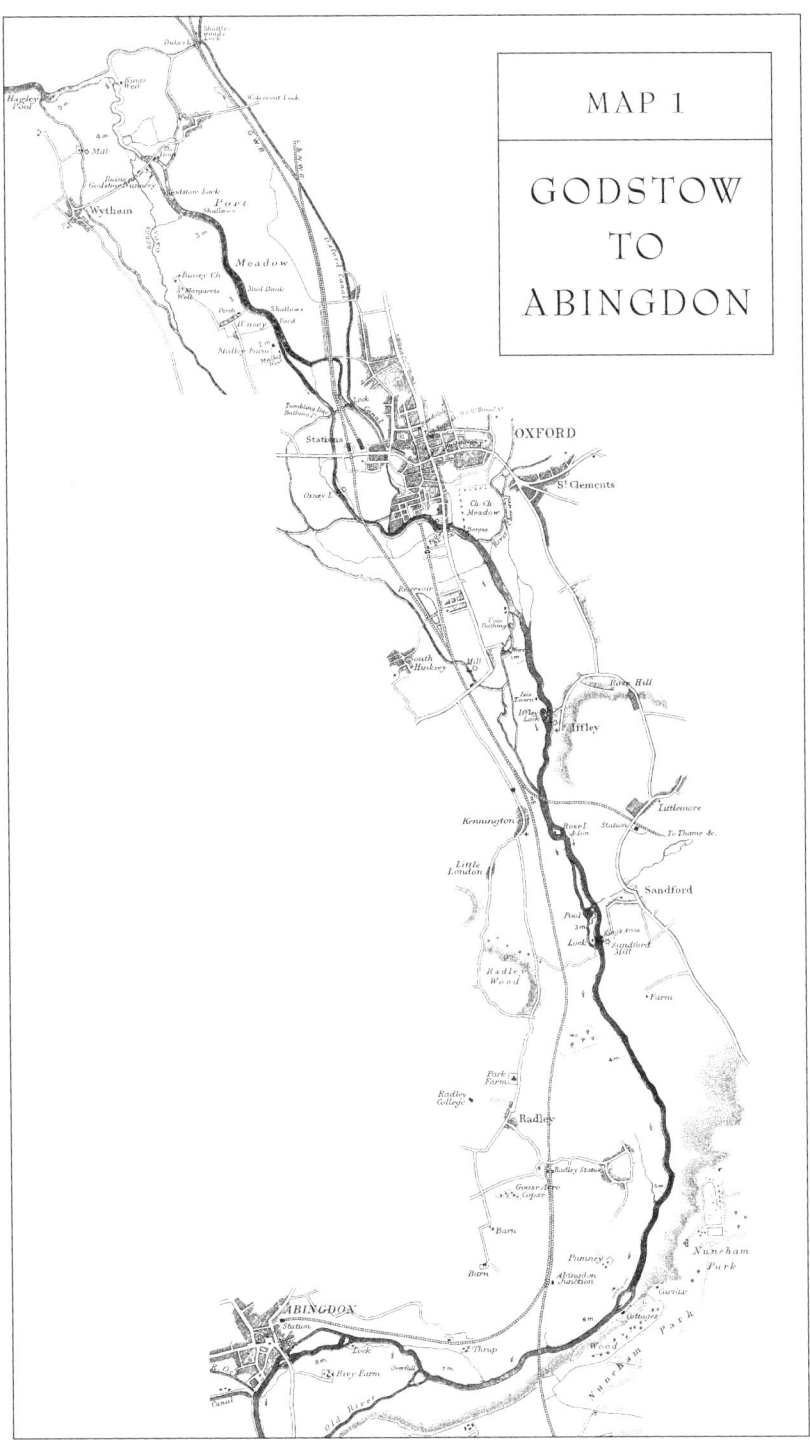

Source: Henry Taunt's *New Map of the River Thames* (ed. 3) 1879, surveyed 1878.

MAP 2

GODSTOW AND PORT MEADOW

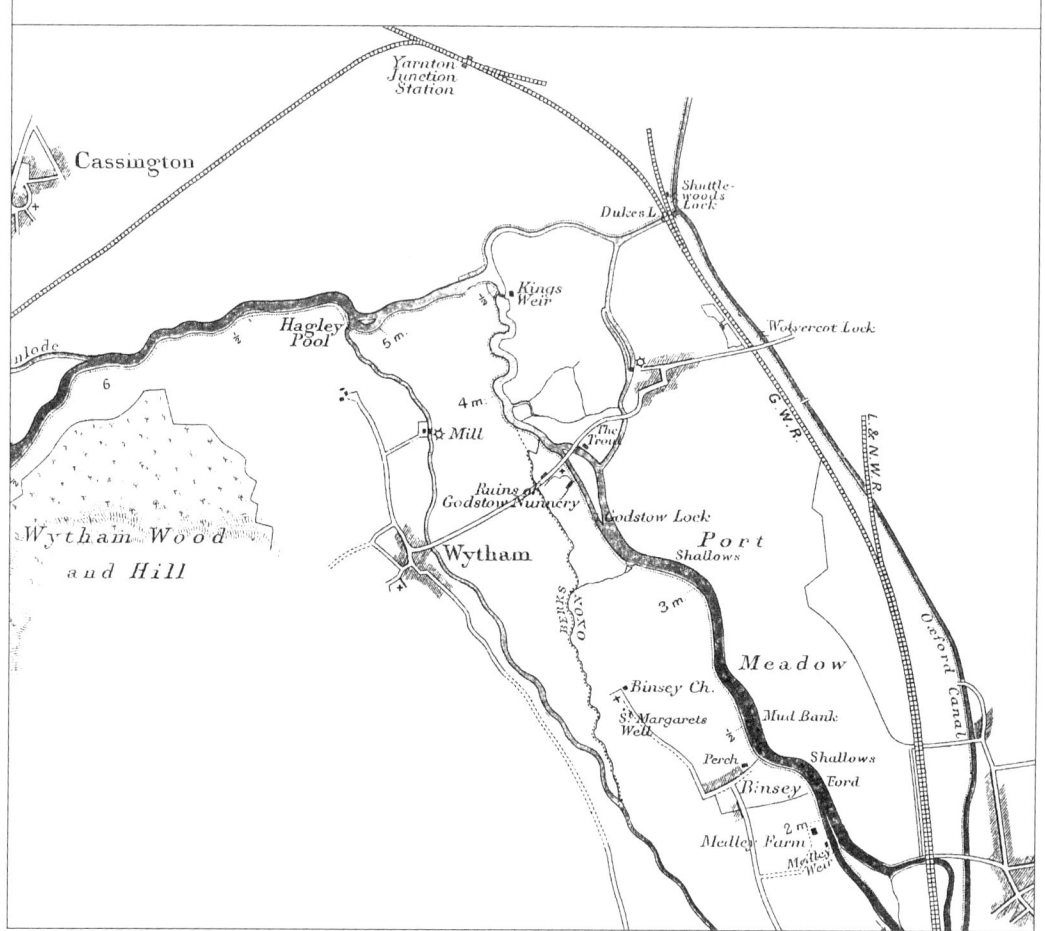

Source: Henry Taunt's *New Map of the River Thames* (ed. 3) 1879, surveyed 1878.

1

GODSTOW

1. 'The Thames, near Godstow' from Alfred Rimmer's *Pleasant Spots Around Oxford* (1878).

19 MAY 1857

Walked with Skeffington* to Godstow, where, oddly enough, I do not remember ever being before.

3 JULY 1862 (Thurs.)

Atkinson and I went to lunch at the Deanery, after which we were to have gone down the river with the children, but as it rained, we remained to hear some music and singing instead. The three sang 'Sally come up' with great spirit. Then croquêt, at which Duckworth joined us, and he and Atkinson[†] afterwards dined with me. I mark this day with a white stone.[‡]

4 JULY 1862 (Fri.)

Duckworth and I made an expedition up the river to Godstow with the three Liddells: we had tea on the bank there, and did not reach Ch. Ch. again till quarter past 8.

ON THE OPPOSITE PAGE, IN A NOTE DATED 10 FEB. 1863:

On which occasion I told them the fairy-tale of "Alice's Adventures Under Ground," which I undertook to write out for Alice, and which is now finished (as to the text) though the pictures are not yet nearly done.

---

* Skeffington Dodgson (1836–1919) was Carroll's younger brother, at this time studying and residing at Christ Church, as too was the next brother in age, Wilfred (1838–1914). By 'Godstow' he means the ruined twelfth-century nunnery on the west bank of the Thames presumably. On the eastern side of the river is The Trout public house. Both buildings feature prominently in the early history of another other-worldly Oxford heroine: Philip Pullman's Lyra (in *La Belle Sauvage*, 2017).

† Francis Home Atkinson (1840–1901) was from Cambridge, and visiting only for Commemoration.

‡ Carroll applied the term 'white stone' to days of outstanding significance. The phrase was used in ancient Rome, and also occurs in the Bible (Revelations 2:17). His first usage was on the day that he purchased his first camera and lens in London, on 18 March 1856. The fictional Tom Brown considered his arrival at Rugby School, aged nine, a 'white stone day' (*Tom Brown's Schooldays*, 1857).

3 AUG. 1862 (Sun.)

Went over to the Deanery to ask if they could come with us to Nuneham on Wednesday, as Harcourt* was writing to his relations at Nuneham House, and found the children at dinner, at which I joined them.

6 AUG. 1862 (Wed.)

In the afternoon Harcourt and I took the three Liddells up to Godstow, where we had tea: we tried the game of "the Ural Mountains" on the way, but it did not prove very successful, and I had to go on with my interminable fairy-tale of "Alice's Adventures". We got back soon after 8.

A very enjoyable expedition, the last, I should think, to which Ina is likely to be allowed to come (her 14th time†).

13 NOV. 1862

Began writing the fairy-tale for Alice, which I told them July 4, going to Godstow. I hope to finish it by Xmas.

13 SEPT. 1864

At Croft.‡ Finished drawing the pictures in the MS. copy of "Alice's Adventures".

---

* Augustus George Vernon Harcourt (1834–1919) was the nephew of William Vernon Harcourt (1789–1871), owner of the manor of Nuneham, a popular destination for boating parties on the Thames several miles downstream (see page 97).

† This three-word addition reveals that nine boat trips with Alice's older sister Lorina, always known as Ina, remain undisclosed. The first ever with her was on 5 June 1856, when she had just turned seven. Alice's first known river trip was on 26 May 1862 (see page 76), though she had certainly been on others before this.

‡ Croft was the village in Yorkshire where Carroll's father was vicar from 1843 to 1868.

2. Godstow (c1880), looking north, and showing The Trout public house and the bridge which takes the road westwards to Wytham over the Thames. (*Oxfordshire History Centre*)

> July 4 (F) Atkinson brought over to my rooms some friends of his, a Mrs + Miss Peters, of whom I took photograph + who afterwards looked over my album + staid to lunch. They then went off to the Museum, + Duckworth + I made an expedition up the river to Godstow with the 3 Liddells : we had tea on the bank there, + did not reach Ch. Ch. again till ¼ past 8, when we took them on to my rooms to see my collection of micro-photographs, + restored them to the Deanery, just before 9

3. Extract from Charles Dodgson's diary for 4 July 1862 (from *Mr Dodgson,* The Lewis Carroll Society, 1973; the original is at the British Library).

GODSTOW

It was on the bank of the Thames near the hamlet of Godstow, some three miles north of Oxford, that the phenomenon of 'Alice' had its birth. Here it was, on Friday 4 July 1862, that the Oxford don Charles Lutwidge Dodgson (1832–1898), later to achieve worldwide fame as Lewis Carroll, and Robinson Duckworth of Trinity College (1834–1911) enjoyed a picnic with three young sisters called Liddell. They had rowed upstream that day from the Oxford college of Christ Church, where Carroll lived and worked and where the girls – Lorina (aged 13), Alice (10), and Edith (8) – resided as daughters of the Dean, Henry Liddell.* There was nothing especially unusual about this particular fivesome going out on the river together; nor was it out of the ordinary for Carroll to invent stories that day to keep the girls amused. But the date is enshrined in the history of children's literature as the one when Alice persuaded the versatile mathematics don to write down for her the impromptu story that he had begun earlier that day.

Carroll's immediate diary comment that day was brief and unremarkable: 'Duckworth and I made an expedition up the river to Godstow with the three Liddells: we had tea on the bank there.' It is his later addition which defines the day's supreme significance: 'On which occasion I told them the fairy-tale of "Alice's Adventures Underground," which I undertook to write out for Alice.' The other titles that he had considered are also noted: 'Alice's Hour in Elfland' (9 June 1864); and 'Alice's Adventures in Wonderland' (28 June 1864). He stuck with 'Under Ground' in the handwritten manuscript that he presented to Alice on 26 November 1864, emphasising the importance of the day with his subtitle

---

* Henry George Liddell (1811–98) was a former graduate of Christ Church. He married Lorina Reeve (1826–1910) in 1846, the year that he became headmaster of Westminster School, and moved into the Deanery at Christ Church in 1855, joined early the following year by his wife and family.

of 'A Christmas Gift to a Dear Child in Memory of a Summer Day'. It was an expanded version of this original offering that was published as *Alice's Adventures in Wonderland*, when the importance of the 4 July was further accentuated by the date selected for publication: 4 July 1865.

There are three first-hand accounts of the circumstances of that Friday. Carroll himself wrote in April 1887, within a review of the first adaptation of 'Alice' for the stage the previous December:

> Many a day had we rowed together on that quiet stream – the three little maidens and I – and many a fairy tale had been extemporised for their benefit … yet none of those many tales got written down: they lived and died, like summer midges, each in its own 'golden afternoon,' until there came a day when, as it chanced, one of my little listeners petitioned that the tale might be written out for her.*

In *The Lewis Carroll Picture Book*, edited by Carroll's nephew and first biographer, Stuart Dodgson Collingwood, he reprinted a letter from Robinson Duckworth,† written about 1897, giving his recollection of 'the famous Long Vacation voyage to Godstow' with Carroll, stating that 'I rowed *stroke* and he rowed *bow* … and the story was actually composed and spoken over my *shoulder* for the benefit of Alice Liddell, who was acting as "cox" of our gig'.

Alice herself ventured only two main printed recollections, both via her son, Caryl Hargreaves (1887–1955). These were in the *New York Times* of 1 May 1932 and the *Cornhill Magazine* of July 1932, when she was 80 years old, and had been invited to America on account of the centenary of the birth of Charles Dodgson. In the latter periodical she emphasised the privileged nature of the role referred to by Duckworth, that of the cox:

> Sometimes (a treat of great importance in the eyes of the fortunate one) one of us was allowed to take the tiller ropes: and, if the course was a

---

* *The Theatre*, April 1887, p180.
† Robinson Duckworth (1834–1911) was a fellow of Trinity College from 1860 to 1876, and a Canon of Westminster from 1875. In 1866 he had been appointed as personal tutor to Queen Victoria's youngest son, Prince Leopold, and was his governor until 1870.

little devious, little blame was accorded to the small but inexperienced coxswain.*

Alice also affirmed that Duckworth was most often the other adult on these rowing trips, and that: 'We went on the river for the afternoon with Mr. Dodgson … at most four or five times every summer term.' Most of these journeys took them downstream from Christ Church. The outing of 4 July 1862 was unusual in that they went up the river. Of the many boating trips which Carroll noted between the first on 5 June 1856 and last on 25 June 1863 (bearing in mind that his journal for April 1858 to May 1862 is missing), only two were to Godstow, or indeed anywhere upstream of Christ Church. In the *New York Times* piece, Caryl added that Alice's 'memories of him are not only of an inexhaustible flow of the most delightful fairy tales (usually illustrated as he went along by quaint pencil or ink drawings on any handy bit of paper) but also of extemporized songs and rhymes which were even more fun'.†

One of the children whom Carroll befriended later in life, Isa Bowman (1874–1958), wrote soon after his death a detailed account of the time she spent in his company. Her informed understanding was that

> The story, often continued on many summer afternoons, sometimes in the cool Christ Church rooms, sometimes in a slow gliding boat in a still river between banks of rushes and strange bronze and yellow waterflowers, or sometimes in a great hay-field, with the insects whispering in the grass all round, grew in its conception and idea.‡

The only other known trip to Godstow came a month later, on 6 August 1862, when Augustus Harcourt, another Christ Church academic, was the other adult. On this occasion, Carroll attempted to amuse the girls with a game, but then had to accede to their requests 'to go on with my interminable fairy-tale', which he was already referring to as 'Alice's

---

* *Cornhill Magazine*, July 1932, p8.
† *New York Times*, 1 May 1932, p7.
‡ Isa Bowman, *The Story of Lewis Carroll* (1889) p112.

Adventures'. It may be significant that these two Godstow trips are the only ones when any specific reference is made by Carroll to story-telling. A possible conclusion is that this route – initially past the working-class suburb of St Ebbe's, the city gas-works, and the developing suburb of Osney Town – presented fewer diversions for the children. Downstream from Christ Church the banks of the Thames were (and still are to this day) almost instantly rural in nature, there were places to stop for refreshments, and the river might well have presented scenes of a generally busier and more entertaining nature.

So it may well have been the comparatively unremarkable nature of the Thames upstream of Christ Church – as far as the girls were concerned, anyway – which was an important factor in the creation of 'Alice' on Friday 4 July 1862. If so, it was a very near thing altogether. Carroll's original intention had been to go *down* the river the day before. Had it not rained that particular Thursday they would have taken that preferred and seemingly more stimulating route, with probably fewer opportunities for story-telling. Godstow had not been the first choice for the outing in August either; again Nuneham had initially been the intended destination.

The weather on 4 July 1862 has been much debated, since the participants' memories are at odds with the Meteorological Office's record of the day as 'cool and rather wet'. The Radcliffe Observatory in Oxford recorded 'rain after 2pm, cloud cover 10/10, and maximum shade temperature of 67.9 degrees',* and *Jackson's Oxford Journal* of 12 July 1862 recorded figures (from the same Radcliffe Observatory source) of: 0.175 inches of rain and a mean temperature of 54.8 degrees. Yet Carroll's recollection in 1887 was:

Full many a year has slipped away, since that 'golden afternoon' that gave thee birth, but I can call it up almost as clearly as if it were yesterday – the cloudless blue above, the watery mirror below, the boat drifting idly on

---

* Gardner, p9/10. Nor could they have confused the day with their other known up-river journey, on 6 August 1862, because on that similarly completely overcast day the figures were: 0.527 inches of rain and a mean temperature of 57.7 degrees (*Jackson's*, 9 August 1862).

its way, the tinkle of the drops that fell from the oars, as they waved so sleepily to and fro, and (the one bright gleam of life in all this slumberous scene) the three eager faces, hungry for news of fairy-land, and who would not be said 'nay' to: from whose lips 'tell us a story, please,' had all the stern immutability of Fate!*

Alice's memory of the day was similar: 'Nearly all of *Alice's Adventures Underground* was told on that blazing summer afternoon with the heat haze shimmering over the meadows where the party landed to shelter for awhile in the shadow cast by the haycocks near Godstow.'† In the *Cornhill* article she observed: 'Many of my earlier adventures must be irretrievably lost to posterity, because Mr. Dodgson told us many, many stories before the famous trip on the river to Godstow.' More than thirty years earlier, in *Life and Letters*, the hastily produced first biography of Carroll, his nephew Stuart Dodgson Collingwood provided a short verbatim paragraph in which he quoted Alice as saying, 'Most of Mr. Dodgson's stories were told to us on river expeditions to Nuneham and Godstow' and

> I believe the beginning of 'Alice' was told one summer afternoon when the sun was so burning that we had landed in the meadows down‡ the river, deserting the boat to take refuge in the only bit of shade to be found, which was under a new-made hayrick. Here from all three came the old petition of 'Tell us a story,' and so began the ever-delightful tale.

And so, no matter if the 'cloudless blue' sky and 'blazing summer afternoon' were actually recollections of another day entirely, from the riverside reality of that day came the opening line of prose from *Alice's Adventures in Wonderland* – 'Alice was beginning to get very tired of sitting by her sister on the bank, and of having nothing to do' – followed immediately by Alice's impulsive pursuit of the White Rabbit into his burrow. Of this crucial beginning, Carroll wrote: 'I distinctly

---

* *The Theatre*, April 1887, p181.
† *Cornhill Magazine*, July 1932, p8.
‡ Collingwood, p96. Alice's use of 'down' the river, when Godstow is 'up', must have been habitual (being the direction in which they were all much more accustomed to go) rather than a faulty or conflicting memory.

remember ... I had sent my heroine straight down a rabbit-hole, to begin with, without the least idea what was to happen afterwards."* What did happen afterwards, of course, is that the story became among the most famous ever told ...

∾ TEXTS ∾

The essential role played by the Thames in the creation of 'Alice' is apparent in the introductory poem in *Alice's Adventures in Wonderland*. The 'Three' referred to are Lorina, Alice, and Edith, hence the presumed play on words of 'little' and 'Liddell':

> **All in the golden afternoon**
> **Full leisurely we glide;**
> **For both our oars, with little skill,**
> **By little arms are plied,**
> **While little hands make vain pretence**
> **Our wanderings to guide.**
>
> **Ah, cruel Three! In such an hour,**
> **Beneath such dreamy weather,**
> **To beg a tale of breath too weak**
> **To stir the tiniest feather!**
> **Yet what can one poor voice avail**
> **Against three tongues together?**

The penultimate verse reads:

> **Thus grew the tale of Wonderland:**
> **Thus slowly, one by one,**
> **Its quaint events were hammered out –**
> **And now the tale is done,**
> **And home we steer, a merry crew,**
> **Beneath the setting sun.**

---

* *The Theatre*, April 1887, p180.

4. Tenniel's 'Father William', balancing an eel, in the *Wonderland* chapter called 'Advice from a Caterpillar'. In the background are three 'bucks' (wicker eel traps), once a common sight at weirs in the Oxford area.

5. Carroll's own drawing of the same scene in 'Alice's Adventures under Ground'.

In *Through the Looking-Glass* (1872) there are two poems, both demonstrating that, despite a gap of many years, the river trips were still foremost in Carroll's mind. The introductory poem includes the lines:

> **A tale begun in other days,**
> **When summer suns were glowing –**
> **A simple chime, that served to time**
> **The rhythm of our rowing.**

The final lines are:

> **And though the shadow of a sigh**
> **May tremble through the story,**
> **For 'happy summer days' gone by,***
> **And vanish'd summer glory –**
> **It shall not touch with breath of bale**
> **The pleasance of our fairy-tale.**

Alice's middle name of Pleasance is also incorporated into the acrostic poem (the first letter of each line spelling 'Alice Pleasance Liddell') at the end of *Looking-Glass*. It begins:

> **A BOAT, beneath a summer sky,**
> **Lingering onward dreamily**
> **In an evening of July –**
>
> **Children three that nestle near,**
> **Eager eye and willing ear,**
> **Pleased a simple tale to hear.**

The final verse reads:

> **Ever drifting down the stream –**
> **Lingering in the golden gleam –**
> **Life, what is it but a dream?**†

---

* In quotes because 'happy summer days' are the last three words of *Wonderland*.

† A popular contemporary tune (probably adapted from an American minstrel song, first appearing in printed form in 1852) was: 'Row, row, row, your boat | Gently down the stream. | Merrily, merrily, merrily, merrily, | Life is but a dream.'

2

PORT MEADOW

6. 'Barges at Binsey' from Alfred J. Church's *Isis and Thamesis* (1886). In fact, the scene shown is not Binsey, but Medley, where the Thames splits into two at the southern end of Port Meadow. The easterly branch shown flows onwards through the city as the Castle Mill Stream, of which the Trill Mill Stream (see Chapter 7) is an offshoot. The houseboats, belonging to the rival families of boat-hirers called Beesley (far bank) and Bossom, were among Oxford's first floating homes.

8 JUNE 1863

Review of the Oxford and Cambridge Volunteers in Port Meadow, after which each company gave dinner to a Cambridge company, Ch. Ch. taking one.

24 JUNE 1863 (Wed.)

Great Volunteer Review in Port Meadow. I went there with Dukes (who had to leave before it was over) and there I fell in with the Liddells, and with Hoole.* We waited to see them safe off, and walked back, and dined in my rooms.

---

*   Charles Holland Hoole (1837–1902), a Christ Church don.

7. Tenniel's King's horses and King's men in the *Looking-Glass* chapter called 'The Lion and the Unicorn'.

PORT MEADOW

Between Godstow and Oxford lies Port Meadow, some 350 acres of river floodplain, bordered by the Thames on the west and the railway to the east. Its appearance, save a southern section which has been elevated through past use as a depository for the city's refuse, is much as it would have looked to the party which rowed up the river here in July 1862. The meadow has been a place of resort for Oxonians for centuries, hosting many social and sporting events, of which horse-races were of especial note, from the seventeenth century onwards.

One of *the* Oxford events of 1863 was held on Port Meadow. This was the Great Volunteer Review, a 'sham fight' involving 8,000 men from 'some of the finest bodies of cavalry, artillery, and infantry in the country', as Oxford's weekly newspaper *Jackson's Oxford Journal* described it. An estimated (but surely wildly exaggerated) 40,000 to 50,000 people watched the spectacle on 24 June. Carroll was among them, likewise the Liddell family, perhaps in the grandstand erected specially for the occasion at the top (northern) end. If so, they may have been disappointed, as it evidently did not provide the expected advantages. *Jackson's* commented: 'It is hardly to be wondered at that the occupants of this stand should express themselves in terms of great dissatisfaction, in witnessing less of the movements than many persons who had paid nothing.' However, 'another stand, erected on another part of the ground by Mr. C. Bossom,* found a good number of patrons; barges were moored in the river, on which further accommodation

---

* The Bossom family's association with the river in Oxford goes back centuries. In the second half of the nineteenth century, they and a rival family called Beesley operated boat-hire facilities at Medley, on the western edge of Port Meadow, and were among the first people in Oxford to make their boats permanent homes. The current boat-building firm at Medley still (2022) trades under the Bossom name. A more complete history of the colourful Bossom and Beesley families of Oxford appears in *A Towpath Walk in Oxford* (see the advertisement at the end of this book).

was provided ... The manoeuvres were brought to a close at about six o'clock.'*

However much or little they saw, the excitement of the event seems likely to have been fresh in everyone's mind the next day, when Carroll escorted the whole Liddell family on a momentous river trip to Nuneham (see page 98). The chaotic battle scenes in *Looking-Glass* may be reminiscent of the occasion, as the conditions could well have introduced an element of pantomime: 'masses of human beings covered terra firma – if the Meadow, which, owing to the late rains, was in some places exceedingly swampy, may be so designated'. There was early confusion, when an 'ugly rush' meant that 'troops and spectators seemed almost inextricably intermingled. Chaos, however, was soon reduced to order.' Military exercises also took place within the grounds of Nuneham Park at this time, though, and might also have been witnessed by Carroll and the Liddells, given their familiarity with the location and with the Harcourt family.

Alice was familiar with Port Meadow from a recreational perspective too, recalling in *Cornhill Magazine* that a 'great joy was to go out riding with my father ... on Port Meadow, or go to Abingdon through Radley, and there were the most lovely rides through Wytham Woods' (see Map 1).

∾ TEXT ∾

In the *Looking-Glass* chapter called 'The Lion and the Unicorn' the White King asks Alice: 'Did you happen to see any soldiers, my dear, as you came through the wood?' Could her response of 'Yes, several thousand, I should think' have been inspired by the Great Volunteer Review of 24 June 1863? Having just left Humpty Dumpty, and heard an

---

* In *Looking-Glass,* Tweedledum and Tweedledee 'fight till six, and then have dinner'.

ominous 'heavy crash', Alice had watched the King's men and the King's horses pass. First the soldiers

came running through the wood, at first in twos and threes, then ten or twenty together, and at last in such crowds that they seemed to fill the whole forest. Alice ... thought that in all her life she had never seen soldiers so uncertain on their feet: they were always tripping over something or other, and whenever one went down, several more always fell over him, so that the ground was soon covered with little heaps of men. Then came the horses. Having four feet, these managed rather better than the foot-soldiers: but even *they* stumbled now and then; and it seemed to be a regular rule that, whenever a horse stumbled, the rider fell off instantly.

8. Sketch of Alice Liddell, aged eight, copied by Carroll from his photograph on page 107.

9. Medley, looking north. Henry Taunt's photograph of about 1880 shows the rival boat-hire firms of Bossom (left) and Beesley (right), with the wide expanse of Port Meadow in the distance. (*Oxfordshire History Centre*)

10. (opposite) 'From the Thames, near Binsey-Green', first published (Charles Knight, London) in *The Land We Live In*, March 1848. The view was especially chosen because it had 'seldom, if ever, before been engraved'. In the middle ground is Port Meadow, on the far side of the river, which is apparently crossed here by a ford. It was not until 1865 that the present footbridge across the main river was installed, providing pedestrian access to Medley Manor and Binsey.

3

BINSEY

9 MAY 1875 (Sun.)

Re-opening of Binsey Church, which prevented Prout meeting me on the hill as usual.*

11 MAY 1879 (Sun.)

I record, as remarkable, what Prout tells me – that his thermometer last night registered 30°, and that yesterday morning the wagtails were running about on the ice on Binsey green!

4 JUNE 1881 (Sat.)

As Prout was sent for yesterday to his brother in London (who died) Salwey undertook to take the service at Binsey for him, and I volunteered to help him, and prepared a short sermon. But I am not destined to deliver it, as Prout returned this evening. It is some relief to one's nerves, as I was looking forwards with terror to the ordeal. It is years since I have tried preaching.†

---

* Thomas Jones Prout (1823–1909) was a lifelong friend of Carroll who entered Christ Church in 1842, having been educated under Henry Liddell at Westminster School. Like Carroll he remained in residence at Christ Church his whole life.

† Although ordained as a deacon in 1861, Carroll officiated at church services only rarely, on account of his speech impediment, hence his feeling of 'terror'. The potential stand-in was Herbert Salwey (1842–1929), Christ Church tutor and censor.

BINSEY

Binsey is a hamlet of a dozen or so houses on the opposite (western) side of the Thames to Port Meadow. It forms part of the estate of Carroll's college of Christ Church, which appointed curates to the church there. Carroll's two diary references to Binsey come as a result of his lifelong friendship with Thomas Jones Prout, who held the living of the village's church of St Margaret from 1857 until 1891.

It was Prout who restored a well in the graveyard which had been revered for centuries as the site of the spring miraculously summoned by Oxford's patron saint, Frideswide, early in the eighth century. The reputed healing properties of the well's waters are supposed to have attracted huge numbers of pilgrims, and there is good reason to think that this is the well to which the Dormouse refers at the 'Mad Tea-Party' in *Wonderland*. The three sisters at the bottom of the treacle well clearly represent the three Liddells: 'Elsie', or L. C., is Lorina Charlotte; 'Lacie' is an anagram of Alice; and 'Tillie' is short for Matilda, the pet-name given to Edith. The notion of a treacle well seems at first preposterous, yet is based on an early meaning of the word as a healing liquid or medicine (from the Greek *Thēriakē* meaning 'antidote'). So there was indeed a kind of treacle well at Binsey, and the fictional Alice – who at first declared: 'There is no such thing!' – was wise eventually to admit that 'I dare say there may be *one*'. It is at the 'Mad Tea-Party' that the date of Alice's adventures is revealed as 4 May, which was Alice Liddell's actual birthday. The fictional Alice must be seven years old that day, because she tells the White Queen in *Looking-Glass*, which is clearly set on 4 November, that she is seven-and-a-half years old 'exactly'. The real Alice would have been seven on 4 May 1859. What a pity it is that 1859 is one of the years in Carroll's two missing journals!

In *The Book of the Thames* (1859), Samuel Carter and Anna Maria

Hall recorded their river journey from source to sea. This was the scene at Binsey, at exactly the time when Thomas Prout first assumed responsibility as curate:

> Its church has a heart-broken look; and of the well there is but an indication – a large earth-mound in a corner of the graveyard completely dried up, there being no sign of water; the spring is lost; and so, indeed, is its memory – for we inquired in vain among the neighbouring peasantry for St. Margaret's Well, of which they had heard and knew nothing – *sic transit!*

Under Prout the fortunes of both the church and well improved in the years that followed. St Margaret's Well was restored in 1874, causing the Halls to amend their opinion in the second edition of *The Book of the Thames* (1877) to: 'the ancient and very venerable Well – so long "lost" – has recently been discovered, and water is drawn from it by all the neighbours'. A tongue-in-cheek alternative to the well's new Latin inscription, 'having regard for its proximity to the church', was suggested as:

> When you open your pew-door,
> This may comfort supply
> Should the sermon be dry.[*]

It is, of course, a joke Carroll incorporated into the Mouse's 'Long Tale', where reciting British history from William the Conqueror onwards is deemed 'the driest thing I know'. The friendship between Carroll and Prout is probably sufficient to justify the veiled allusion to the Binsey 'treacle well'. Meanwhile, Prout's reputation for dozing off during the long Christ Church meetings satisfactorily explains why it is a sleepy Dormouse who relates the story. Carroll was not averse to poking fun at his friends. The diary of Thomas Vere Bayne (1829–1908), another Christ Church colleague, whom Carroll had known since his childhood in Cheshire, includes four limericks composed by Carroll in about 1856.

---

[*] Andrew Clark, editor of *Survey of the Antiquities of the City of Oxford, composed in 1661–6, by Anthony Wood* I. (1889) p329.

Although no actual names are included, the subjects are quite clear, including this one:

> An unfortunate Tutor named [Prout]
> Never knew what he lectured about;
> When they said "What's that word"?
> He seemed not to have heard,
> But in Liddell and Scott looked it out.[*]

Many Carroll commentators have suggested another reason for his inclusion of the Binsey 'treacle well': that Mary Prickett (1832–1920), Alice's governess, was from the village. Prickett is a fairly unusual name, and the family had indeed been present in Binsey since at least the sixteenth century. Mary Prickett, however, was not from this line of the family – despite Carroll having provided several other apparent indicators.

Carroll never acknowledged any real-life inspiration for his characters, but he seems to have come very close when describing the Red Queen as 'a Fury, … cold and calm; … formal and strict, yet not unkindly; pedantic to the tenth degree, the concentrated essence of all governesses!'.[†] In the chapter called 'The Garden of Live Flowers', the Rose calls the Red Queen 'one of the thorny kind'. This, surely, was an allusion to the children's nickname for their governess of 'Pricks'[‡] but additionally, given Carroll's love of wordplay, there is reason to think that he was combining a pun on 'Thornbury', the ancient name for the site of St Margaret's Church and Well, with the Prickett family's long association with the locality.[§]

It is interesting to note that the phrase 'thorny kind' was used only in

---

[*] See Appendix 5 for the other three limericks. This is the first publication of all four. 'Liddell and Scott' refers to the authoritative Greek–English Lexicon published by Henry George Liddell and Robert Scott in 1843.

[†] *The Theatre*, April 1887, p182.

[‡] *Cornhill Magazine*, July 1932, p1.

[§] This presumed additional clue was first proposed in 2001, in my first edition of *A Towpath Walk in Oxford* (see the advertisement at the end of this book). The Red Queen's rapid increase in size is interesting too. 'It's the fresh air that does it,' says the Rose, and 'wonderfully fine air it is, out here'. It seems just the kind of thing a local of Binsey might say, given Oxford's reputation for a dank and enervating climate.

the first edition. In the second of 1878 it was changed to 'one of the kind that has nine spikes'. Had Carroll recognised that he had been just a little too obvious? Or had he realised by then that in fact Mary Prickett had no obvious connection with Binsey after all? Because despite these apparent clues, she was not descended from the Binsey Pricketts at all. Her father, James, was born in Oxford, but his father, and all the identifiable generations preceding, had come from the Oxfordshire town of Thame. It is certainly not impossible that there was some genealogical connection, and Mary actually was related to the Binsey Pricketts, or assumed that she was, or Carroll did. Yet the evidence of any such family relationship remains unproven (see Appendix 1). Whatever, it is certainly not true, as many texts claim, that Mary Prickett or her father came from the village.

Prout was still the incumbent at Binsey when Andrew Clark visited on 25 October 1887, observing that he found that the well was 'in better condition' than previously and that 'the churchyard was tidily fenced and very neatly kept', and with 'the surface of the water being about six feet below the level of the ground'.*

Little has changed subsequently (apart from the constant audio-intrusion of traffic on the A34) and the peculiar, timeless ambience of the location was well demonstrated by the experience of a visitor in the 1960s, who suggested in *Country Life* that the churchyard must be haunted because a dog, which normally followed him everywhere without fail, absolutely refused to enter on two occasions. The vicar of Binsey at that time, Arnold Mallinson, responded to assure the magazine's readers (11 April 1963) that the dog 'was not deterred by ghosts, for there are none there, but by perception of the powerful holiness of the place occasioned by the existence of the well of St. Margaret'. In the same letter he claimed: 'When the Rev. Mr. Prout restored the well in the 19th century he asked Lewis Carroll about it. Lewis advised, "Leave WELL alone!"' This, of course, is wordplay that Carroll employed in his text,

---

* Andrew Clark in *Survey of the Antiquities of the City of Oxford, composed in 1661–6, by Anthony Wood* I. (1889) p329.

the Dormouse telling Alice that the three sisters were not merely in the well, but 'well in' it! Mallinson's source for this anecdote may have been Prout's great-nephew – in the St Frideswide parish magazine of August 1963 he mentioned having received a letter (untraced) from him 'full of interesting things' – although it might equally have been his 'own invention', so to speak: Mallinson was clearly a little prone to presumption, as shown by his attribution of the creator of the Liddell Door in his own church of St Frideswide, for instance (see Appendix 5).

Mallinson was also one of the first people – if not the very first – to assert that Binsey was *definitely* the site of Carroll's 'treacle well'.[*] This was in the 'St. Frideswide's and St. Margaret's Magazine' of February 1967, where, although clearly not a particular fan – 'the Alice books are sad, bad, beautiful – and boring' – he stated unequivocally: 'The treacle well referred to is ours. In local parlance it still remains, erroneously, as Binsey treacle mine.' Two years earlier James (later Jan) Morris had made a similar, but more tentative connection, wondering if their boat might have been 'passing Binsey as this fancy came to Carroll's mind; for there, so an old Oxford country joke has it, treacle mines are worked.'[†]

Just *how* old was this joke? A correspondent to *Country Life* (29 September 1955) wrote that Binsey 'has the reputation of possessing some mythical treacle mines, and … generations of youngsters have been fooled into taking a mug with them when visiting the village for the first time'. How many generations, one wonders? Certainly enough to stretch back into the nineteenth century, because the *Oxford Times* playfully suggested in 1904 that 'nine-tenths of the population of Oxford' considered Binsey to be 'the centre of a "treacle-mining" district'. Whether or not this Binsey whimsy stretched all the way back to the 1860s, to the time when Carroll was composing 'The Mad Tea-Party', is unclear. Certainly there was no actual *well* at that time: two visits

---

[*] There is no mention at all of Binsey in Derek Hudson's 1954 biography, for instance, nor in Martin Gardner's first edition of *The Annotated Alice* (1960). His revised edition of 1970 does make the connection, however, courtesy of Oxford resident Vivien Greene, wife of the novelist Graham Greene.

[†] *Oxford* (Faber & Faber, London, 1965) p242. Historically, the concept of a 'treacle mine' has occurred in many other parts of England, but with no conclusive rationale.

11. St Frideswide's 'treacle well' in the churchyard of St Margaret's Church, a little north of Binsey village. (*Mark Davies, 2010*)

made by members of the Oxford Architectural and Historical Society prove that, because in March 1870 no well was evident, yet in March 1876, when they were met by Rev. Prout himself, he informed them that 'not long since' some workmen who were 'digging in the western part of the churchyard … came upon a well' which he believed, on the basis of the old accounts, was certainly the one of sacred origin.*

So did Carroll modify an existing local yarn about treacle, or was he the inadvertent instigator of it? Who can tell? Not even Time, on this occasion, probably, despite what the Hatter might like to think.

---

* *Proceedings of Oxford Architectural and Historical Society* II. p191 and III. p274.

∼ TEXT ∼

With help from the Cheshire Cat, Alice finds her way to the March Hare's House, and joins the 'Mad Tea-Party'. When Alice declines to tell a story, the Hare and the Hatter wake up the Dormouse, who begins to tell them about three little sisters who live at the bottom of a well. Alice regularly interrupts the Dormouse with questions, exactly as one might imagine her doing when Carroll was first inventing the story, inspired quite possibly by glimpses of Binsey church across the fields as they rowed past.

> 'What did they live on?' said Alice, who always took a great interest in questions of eating and drinking.
> 'They lived on treacle,' said the Dormouse, after thinking a minute or two...

Alice then asks, for the second time:

> 'Why did they live at the bottom of a well?'
> The Dormouse again took a minute or two to think about it, and then said, 'It was a treacle-well.'

Although the context is bizarre, the logic is undeniable! Alice promises not to interrupt, and the Dormouse continues:

> 'These three little sisters – they were learning to draw, you know –'
> 'What did they draw?' said Alice, quite forgetting her promise.
> 'Treacle,' said the Dormouse, without considering at all, this time.

Alice queries where the treacle is drawn from.

> 'You can draw water out of a water-well,' said the Hatter, 'so I should think you could draw treacle out of a treacle-well – eh, stupid?'
> 'But they were *in* the well,' Alice said to the Dormouse, not choosing to notice this last remark.
> 'Of course they were,' said the Dormouse, – 'well in.'

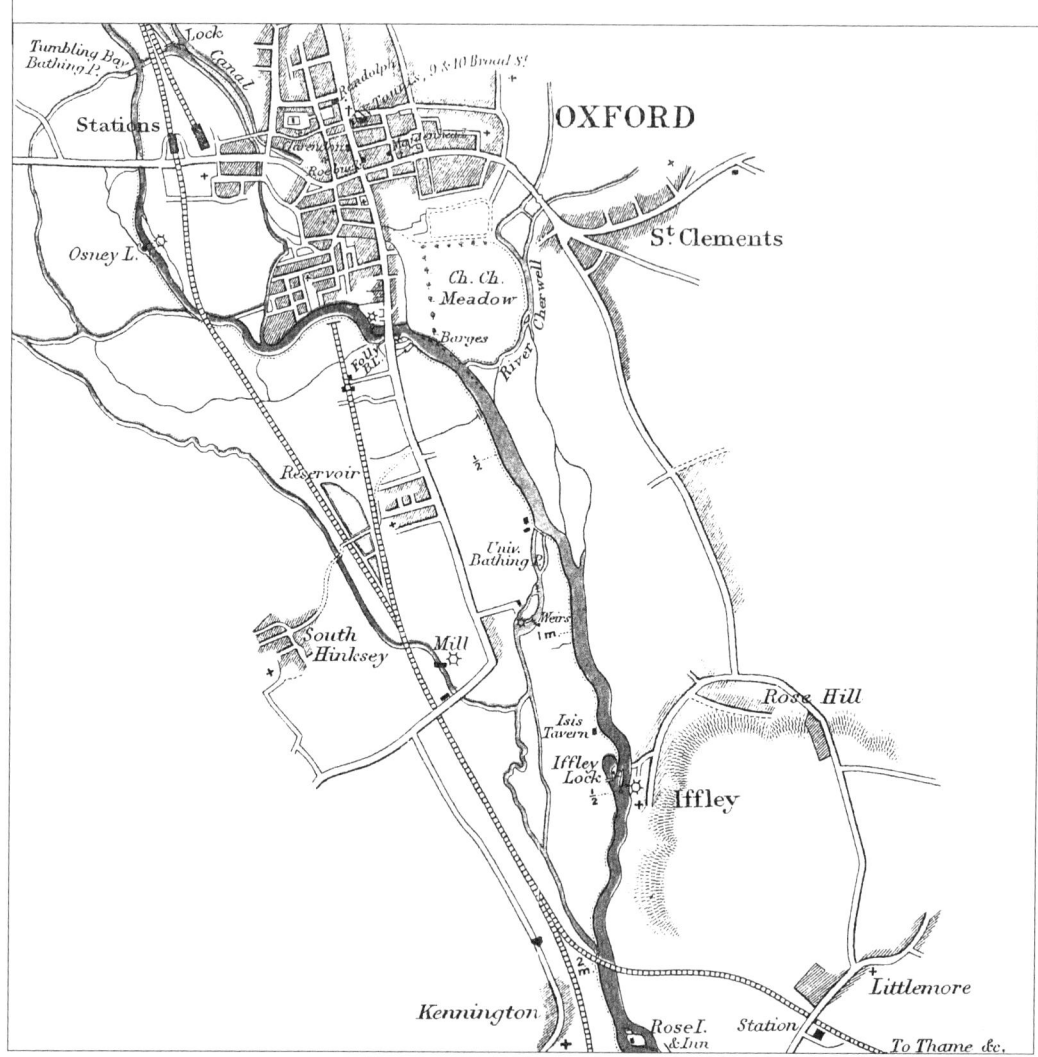

MAP 3

FOUR STREAMS TO ROSE ISLAND

Source: Henry Taunt's *New Map of the River Thames* (ed. 3) 1879, surveyed 1878.

4

JERICHO

12. The Canal Ferry, Jericho from Alfred J. Church's *Isis and Thamesis* (1886). It operated from 1868 for about 100 years.

20 JAN. 1856 (Sun.)

St Paul's in evening with Liddon.*

6 MARCH 1857

Called at the Printing Press and left a note asking Mr. Combe †
if he could tell me where to get a small hand printing-machine.

19 JUNE 1862

To the University Press where we ‡ visited the pictures at
Mr. Combe's.

24 FEB. 1863

In the afternoon I joined the Liddells in their walk (Alice,
Edith and the governess) and went with them to leave a note
at the Press (where I took them to see the printing etc. and
to call on Mrs. Combe, who showed us their pictures), then
to the Museum.§

---

* Henry Parry Liddon (1829–1890). This is Carroll's first mention of St Paul's, almost opposite the Oxford University Press in Jericho. He visited again in November.

† Thomas Combe (1796–1872), Superintendent of Oxford University Press and a great patron of the arts (see page 37), who advised Carroll against any such purchase. Carroll remained on friendly terms with Combe and his wife Martha (1806–1893) throughout their lives.

‡ Carroll had three visitors at this time, lodging in Walton Street, very close to the Press: his maiden aunt Lucy Lutwidge (1805–80) and his two older sisters Frances ('Fanny') Dodgson (1828–1903) and Elizabeth Dodgson (1830–1916). Robinson Duckworth was also one of the party, as he had been two days earlier, when everyone was soaked on the river trip which inspired the 'The Pool of Tears' (see page 90). Lucy Lutwidge assumed a maternal role for the family after the death in 1851 of her sister, Carroll's mother, Frances Jane.

§ Carroll presumably means the Oxford University Museum of Natural History (rather than the Ashmolean), which houses the most complete organic remains anywhere in the world of the extinct dodo and two famous paintings of the bird by Jan Savery (1651) and George Edwards (1758). Is this perhaps where the idea of the Dodo in 'The Pool of Tears' first occurred?

8 MARCH 1863 (Sun.)

Took the afternoon service at Osney Chapel for Chamberlain.*

I was annoyed at finding that I hesitated a good deal in the first Lesson, but I got on better afterwards.

16 JULY 1863

Called on Mr. Combe with my first drawing on wood. Mr. Woolner† was there, just beginning a bust of Mr. Combe. He looked at the drawing (a half length of the heroine) and condemned the arms, which he says I <u>must</u> draw from the life.

19 OCT. 1863

Went to Combe's in the evening to meet the publisher Macmillan and get him to print me some of Blake's 'Songs of Innocence etc.' on large paper.

6 MAY 1864

Sent to the Press a batch of MS. from the first chapter of Alice's Adventures.‡

16 JUNE 1864

Took Holman Hunt.§ Dined at Mr. Combe's to meet him.

---

* Thomas Chamberlain (1811–1892), vicar of St Thomas', and instrumental in the founding of St Frideswide's Church, which is now home to the 'Liddell Door' (see Appendix 5). Chamberlain was a high-profile supporter of Tractarianism and prime mover in the establishment of a Floating Chapel for boatmen in his parish (for more on this celebrated structure, which operated from 1839 to 1868, see *A Towpath Walk in Oxford*).

† Thomas Woolner (1825–1892), the sole Pre-Raphaelite sculptor. Carroll met him again at the Combes' on 17 and 23 July. Woolner's bust of Thomas Combe is at the Ashmolean Museum.

‡ The Oxford University Press Compositors' book includes the costs for 'Dodgson's Fairy Tale' on 6 and 13 May 1864.

§ William Holman Hunt (1827–1910), a founder member of the Pre-Raphaelite Brotherhood.

14 MAY 1865 (Sun.)

Preached for Hackman* at St. Paul's, my first sermon in Oxford, to the largest congregation I have yet addressed, 300 or 400 I should think.

Lunched with Mr. Combe, and met Holman Hunt, Mr. & Mrs. Woolner etc.

2 AUG. 1865

Finally decided on the re-print of 'Alice', and that the first 2000 shall be sold as waste paper. Wrote about it to Macmillan, Combe, and Tenniel.

10 AUG. 1867

Dined with Mr. Penny to meet Mr. and Mrs. Combe and their niece Miss Nathalie.†

25 JULY 1872

Photographed Mr. Combe and Cyril.‡

12 JULY 1876

Edwin went off to the early service at St Barnabas.§

---

* Alfred Hackman (1811–74), Christ Church chaplain 1837–73 and vicar of St Paul's 1844–71. Through Combe, a church warden at St Paul's since 1845, Hackman had first introduced Carroll to Hunt in June 1857.

† This matter-of-fact comment relates to an encounter in Moscow, during Carroll's one and only overseas holiday, an adventure I like to dub 'Alice in Volgaland'. He does not expand on this casual comment, nor does his companion on the trip, Henry Parry Liddon. The niece was probably Mary Henrietta Nattali (born 1839), who was the daughter of Michael Angelo Nattali and Thomas Combe's sister, Helen, who had married in 1826. Robert Penny was the Anglican chaplain.

‡ Cyril Berone Hunt (1866-1934), William Holman Hunt's son. The photograph was taken at Carroll's Christ Church studio, shortly before Combe's death on 29 October.

§ Edwin Dodgson (1846–1918) was Carroll's youngest brother. This is the sole mention of Jericho's St Barnabas' Church in the diaries, although Carroll was among the many subscribers to an endowment fund, contributing £10 towards the target of £2,000 prior to consecration in 1869.

JERICHO

Four Streams marks the point at which two branches of the River Thames, the Bulstake Stream and Sheepwash Channel, meet the main north–south course of the river below Port Meadow. Until the end of the eighteenth century, when Osney Lock was fully opened, these streams constituted part of the main Thames navigation, a meandering route which obliged boats to take a long, troublesome westerly detour (see Map 3).

The Bulstake Stream remained navigable until 1853, when an open-air bathing place called Tumbling Bay was established, but the Sheepwash Channel remains to this day the means by which boats move between the Thames and the Oxford Canal. A little to the north is Jericho, home of Oxford University Press, where the first printing of *Alice* was undertaken in 1865. A slight detour from the main course of the river is therefore appropriate.

En route, anyone straying this way between 1839 and 1868 would almost certainly have noted a very unusual boat moored alongside the canal towpath as it approached the city centre: a Boatmen's Floating Chapel. Although Carroll makes no mention of it in his surviving diaries, it seems improbable that he failed to visit it, either by land or on a short rowing detour, for two main reasons. One is that the Chapel was within St Thomas' parish, which was a Christ Church living, and the other is that his father, Charles (1800–1868), had been instrumental in the establishment of a comparable place of worship on the canal near their old home of Daresbury in Cheshire in the early 1840s. It was one of only ten or so such floating chapels anywhere in the country, designed to encourage boatmen and their families to attend a place of worship where they would feel less conspicuous and self-conscious. When Charles Dodgson was transferred to Croft in Yorkshire in 1843, the *Cheshire*

Chronicle lamented that the 'hitherto well attended and delightful place of worship has been closed for the last two months, chiefly owing to the removal of the Rev. C. Dodgson'.*

When Oxford's Floating Chapel failed to sustain its buoyancy in 1868, it was not revived, presumably because of the imminent opening of the High Anglican church of St Barnabas in the nearby canalside suburb of Jericho. The funds were provided entirely by Thomas Combe (1796–1872), the managing partner of the Bible side of the Oxford University Press from 1851 until his death. Combe has only a passing association with either the river or the canal in Oxford, but his role in enabling the handwritten manuscript presented to one small girl to develop into the phenomenon of 'Alice' is a highly significant one.

Combe lived with his wife Martha (1806–1893) in a large house within the quadrangle of the University Press, which lies in the south-eastern corner of Jericho, closest to the city. Carroll had known the couple since at least early 1857. On 19 October 1863, Thomas Combe introduced Carroll to Alexander Macmillan (1813–96), who subsequently agreed to publish a revised and enlarged version of the handwritten 'Alice's Adventures under Ground' in book form. A few months earlier it was at the Combes' house that Carroll had met the Pre-Raphaelite sculptor Thomas Woolner (1825–92), whose opinion of Carroll's illustrations encouraged the fateful decision ultimately to persuade John Tenniel (1820–1914) to undertake the task. John Ruskin (1819–1900) was another who influenced Carroll's decision, telling him that 'he had not enough talent to make it worth his while to devote much time to sketching'.†

In June 1865, the first 2,000 copies of Alice's *Adventures in Wonderland* were printed at the University Press, and although this first print-run was recalled as substandard, mainly at the insistence of Tenniel, the

---

* See *Canal Boatmen's Missions* by Wendy Freer & Gill Foster, 2004.
† Collingwood, p102. On meeting Ruskin for the first time on 27 October 1857 Carroll's first impression of him was an unflattering 'general feebleness of expression, with no commanding air, or any external signs of deep thought, as one would have expected to see in such a man'. He nonetheless added: 'Dies notabilis'.

book's potential was established, and it was reprinted elsewhere later that year – the whole cost being borne by Carroll himself. At one point, a mischievous publication date of 1 April had been considered, later adjusted to 4 July, exactly three years after the fateful boat trip to Godstow. Of this first printing, Carroll had already inscribed and dispatched 50 copies. Some were probably discarded as worthless soon after, yet the 23 which are known to have survived are now valued, in a down-the-rabbit-hole kind of twist, almost worthy of Wonderland itself, at well over a million pounds each!*

Despite this probable embarrassment for Thomas Combe, he and Carroll seem to have remained on good terms. Carroll continued to dine at the Combes' home at the Press occasionally and often took visitors to view their art collection. The couple were great patrons of the arts, and are especially important for championing the works of the Pre-Raphaelites at a time when these young artists' devotion to naturalistic detail often attracted hostility or ridicule. It was through the Combes that Carroll met artists such as John Everett Millais, William Holman Hunt, and Dante Gabriel Rossetti. The first two often stayed at the Combes' home, producing or completing many of their early paintings there. Through this connection, Carroll, a highly accomplished early photographer, was subsequently able to take pictures of these famous men and their families, in Oxford and in London.

John Ruskin was another key supporter of the Pre-Raphaelites in their early days. A Christ Church graduate, he returned to Oxford in 1869 as the Slade Professor of Fine Art. Soon after this, regretting how infrequently he was able to spend time with the Liddell girls, 'after knowing them from the nursery', he took the opportunity to visit them at the Deanery one evening, when their parents had gone to dine with the Duke and Duchess of Marlborough at Woodstock. 'Alice said that she thought, perhaps, if I would come round after papa and mamma were safe off to Blenheim, Edith and she might give me a cup of tea and

---

* The copy held at the Bodleian Library once belonged to Martha Combe.

13. 'The Observatory and Printing Office' from *A Walk Round Oxford* by Carl Rundt (1802–1868) (c1851). This idealised view of the expanding suburb of Jericho shows (right) the Oxford University Press, where the first copies of *Wonderland* were printed in 1865; (left) the Radcliffe Observatory (1794); and in the centre: Jericho House, from which the suburb took its name, and the Radcliffe Infirmary (1770).

a little singing, and Rhoda show me how she was getting on with her drawing and geometry, or the like.'*

Unfortunately for Ruskin, the snow that winter's night was so deep that the Dean and his wife had to return prematurely. 'Edith had got the tea made, and Alice was just bringing the muffins to perfection' when in marched Mrs Liddell. 'How sorry you must be to see us, Mr. Ruskin!' she said. 'I never was more so,' Ruskin replied. The socially awkward Ruskin was still more sorry a day or two later, when this story was related to the guests at a prestigious dinner he was attending at the Christ Church Deanery. The Princess of Wales was guest of honour, and, as a measure of just how far the story had spread, the narrator, 'perfect in every detail', was Benjamin Disraeli!

Ruskin's ordeal was not over, however. Afterwards, when the Princess was engaged in formal conversation with Ruskin in the drawing room, 'the door from the nurseries opened; and – enter Rhoda – in full dress! Very beautiful!' Disraeli instantly seized the opportunity to increase Ruskin's discomfort:

> Drawing himself to his full height, he advanced to meet Rhoda. The whole room became all eyes and ears. Bowing with kindly reverence, he waved his hand, and introduced her to – the world. 'This is, I understand, the young lady in whose art-education Professor Ruskin is so deeply interested!' And there was nothing for me but simple extinction; for I had never given Rhoda a lesson in my life, (no such luck!), yet I could not disclaim the interest.

John Ruskin's role as the older Liddell girls' teacher appears to be captured in 'The Mock Turtle's Story' in *Looking-Glass*, when the Turtle talks about his education in 'reeling and writhing' (i.e. reading and writing). He says, 'The Drawling-master was an old conger-eel that used to come once a week: he taught us Drawling, Stretching, and Fainting in Coils' (i.e. drawing, sketching, and painting in oils).†

---

* *Præterita* III. (1888) p63–69. Rhoda was Alice's younger sister (1859–1949), whose own artistic talent is demonstrated in the woodcarving of the Liddell Door in St Frideswide's Church, for instance (Image 51).

† Alice and Rhoda were both rewarding pupils: Alice's drawings and watercolours show great skill, as too Rhoda's woodcarving, and that of their younger sister Violet. (Note Carroll's inclusion of a Rose and a Violet in 'The Garden of Live Flowers'.) Their father Henry was also artistically talented, as the numerous blotting paper doodles he made during meetings demonstrates (see Image 23).

14. John and Stephen Salter's premises at Folly Bridge, probably early 1870s, as Stephen Salter retired in 1875. On the far (Oxfordshire) bank of the Thames is the first building that the two brothers occupied in 1858, now The Head of the River public house, next to which the Trill Mill Stream (out of picture) flows into the Thames. The lock (left) was removed in 1884, as part of the same flood-prevention scheme which saw modifications to the River Cherwell's confluence with the Thames (see Chapter 9). (*The Bodleian Library, University of Oxford MS Top. Oxon. d493 f0l29*)

5

FOLLY BRIDGE

The preceding story about John Ruskin has transferred the focus from Jericho and the University Press to Christ Church, omitting a mile and a half of the river, navigated via Osney Lock, to Folly Bridge (see Map 3). In his article for *Cornhill Magazine*, Alice's son, Caryl Hargreaves, prefaced the first-person account of his mother by asking his readers to imagine Carroll and Robinson Duckworth escorting the three Liddell girls from Christ Church 'down to Salter's, where the rowing boats are kept', and to 'watch them choose a nice roomy boat, and plenty of comfortable cushions'. Salter Brothers have been the dominant influence on the river at Folly Bridge, near the probable site of the original Oxen-ford across the Thames, since 1870, the year when they took over the business of local rival, Thomas Hall. Established in 1858, Salters', which built boats as well as hiring them, initially operated from the building which now accommodates The Head of the River pub.* Hall's (see Image 16), on the island opposite, also offered boats for hire, but frequent mentions in Oxford novels suggest that they catered more for competitive oarsmen, and, given their more convenient location, that Salters' would indeed have been Carroll's preferred choice.† Alice's own recollections in the same *Cornhill* article certainly

---

* 'Head of the River' is the term applied to the winning boat at the annual inter-college Eights' Week races (see page 63). The former warehouse was built in 1835/36.
† In *Three Men in a Boat* (1889), Jerome K. Jerome relates wittily how he once pre-arranged the hire of a double sculling skiff, by implication from Oxford, and therefore from Salters'. Despite its encouraging name of *The Pride of the Thames* it turned out to be 'an antediluvian chunk of wood that looked as though it had recently been dug out of somewhere, and dug out carelessly, so as to have been unnecessarily damaged in the process'.

support the idea that they hired a boat, rather than using one owned by the college:

> In the usual way, after we had chosen our boat with great care, we three children were stowed away in the stern, and Mr. Dodgson took the stroke oar. A pair of sculls was always laid in the boat for us little girls to handle when being taught to row by our indulgent host. He succeeded in teaching us in the course of these excursions, and it proved an unending joy to us. When we had learned enough to manage the oars, we were allowed to take our turn at them, while the two men watched and instructed us.

As for the second adult: 'His brother occasionally took an oar in the merry party, but our most usual fifth was Mr. Duckworth, who sang well.' Alice did not distinguish between Skeffington and Wilfred Dodgson, but the latter was by far the more athletic of the two. Neither is named on any of the eleven boat trips logged in Carroll's journals, so presumably Alice must be recalling trips made during the period for which there is no surviving journal: between 1858 and 1862.

Someone else who regularly hired rowing boats from Folly Bridge was John Tenniel, when making a near-annual summer excursion down the river with colleagues from *Punch*. Accounts exist only for the years 1865, 1866, and (probably) 1872, but there were clearly many more, as explained in Appendices 2 and 3. They were joined on the 1865 trip by Charles Dickens junior (1837–1896), whose own enthusiasm for the river is evinced by the many editions of his *Dictionary of the Thames* published from 1879 onwards, and which contained a special section on 'the favourite excursion from Oxford to London'. His father too was not immune to the charms of a river journey. Although other evidence of time spent on the Thames is scarce, in a letter of 27 May 1865 he wrote, 'The journey down from Oxford to Reading, on the Thames, is more charming than one can describe in words. I rowed down last June, through miles upon miles of water lilies, lying on the water close together, like a fairy pavement.'*

---

* *The Letters of Charles Dickens* VIII. (1995) edited by Graham Storey & Kathleen Mary Tillotson, 1995.

15. & 16.
Two illustrations from *The Further Adventures of Mr. Verdant Green* by 'Cuthbert Bede' (1854). The panoramic sketch shows Folly Bridge in the distance and Grandpont House (see Appendix 3) to the far left. Hall & Sherratt (as the name was more usually spelled) operated a boat-hire business at Folly Bridge which was later absorbed by Salter Brothers.

A short walk from Folly Bridge in the direction of the city centre lies Floyd's Row. This is now a side-entrance to Oxford Police Station, but in the nineteenth century it was a cul-de-sac of 26 terraced houses, ending at a branch of the Thames called the Trill Mill Stream. The 1861 and 1871 Censuses show that James and Elizabeth Prickett, the parents of Alice's governess Mary Prickett, lived at No. 12 (see Appendix 1).

17. Folly Bridge, from Mr & Mrs S. C. Hall's *The Book of the Thames* (1859).

6

ALICE'S
SHOP

A little farther into town, on the western side of St Aldate's, is a building which illustrates a 'Waterland' theme as well as any situated closer to the actual river. This is No. 83 St Aldate's, popularly known as the shop drawn by John Tenniel to illustrate the chapter in *Looking-Glass* called 'Wool and Water'. This is an apparently nonsensical episode, with a sheep as a shopkeeper and a sudden transformation of the shop interior into a stream. Yet, in line with much of Carroll's apparent nonsense, it seems likely to have a basis in reality.

The character of the Sheep would seem to have been a shared joke between Alice and Carroll, at the expense of the shopkeeper's wife, who perhaps reminded them of a sheep, in either voice or appearance.* But why the sudden transformation from a shop to a river? A logical explanation for an illogical episode derives from Oxford's age-old vulnerability to flooding. Many are the historical instances of inhabitants of the low-lying parts of the city having to elude flood waters by resorting to their upper rooms, and being obliged to move from house to house by boat.† No. 83 St Aldate's was unlikely to be affected in normal years, but in December

---

* The shopkeepers at No. 83 St Aldate's from at least 1861 (and probably since at least 1851) until 1876 were John (1797–1883) and Mary (1802–1889) Millin (see Appendix 2).
† The earliest example of Oxford as a setting for fiction, Chaucer's *The Miller's Tale*, plays on this theme, with a focus on Osney.

18. Tenniel's 'Wool and Water'
illustrations. The interior of the real shop
at 83 St Aldate's is the reverse of that
shown, as befits a 'looking-glass' view.
The real Alice Liddell had dark hair and
a fringe (see page 107), but Tenniel chose
to give his 'Alice' a look made fashionable
by the Pre-Raphaelite movement.

1852, for instance, Carroll's second winter in Oxford, the flooding was exceptional. The *Illustrated London News* of 4 December reported several drownings and the need to use boats to move passengers to and from the railway station: 'The Cherwell and Isis* are, in extent, more like seas than rivers. All descriptions of property were to be seen floating down the waters, and carcasses of sheep, pigs, and horses, were seen lying in many parts of the country where the water has been drained off.'

This event is incorporated into the novel *The Adventures of Mr. Verdant Green*, set initially in 1852, by Rev. Edward Bradley (1827–89), writing under the name of 'Cuthbert Bede'. Lewis Carroll was a freshman of almost the same vintage as the fictional Verdant Green, a coincidence which makes the novel's factually influenced descriptions especially pertinent.

> One of those inundations occurred to which Oxford is so liable, and the meadow-land to the south and west of the city was covered by the flood. Boats plied to and from the railway station in place of omnibuses; ... the Isis was amplified to the width of Christ Church meadows; the Broad Walk had a peep at itself upside down in the glassy mirror; the windings of the Cherwell could only be traced by the trees on its banks. There was 'Water, water everywhere'; and a disagreeable quantity of it too, as those Christ Church men whose ground-floor rooms were towards the meadows soon discovered.†

It seems certain that if water reached as far as Christ Church, then 'Alice's Shop', situated in a low stretch of St Aldate's, and with its floor below street level, would have been flooded that winter, and probably on other occasions to which Carroll would have been witness: in 1867, for instance, by which time Carroll was beginning to formulate ideas for his sequel. Carroll's friend Henry Parry Liddon noted in his diary on 25 March 1867: 'The floods today higher than have been known in Oxford

---

* The Isis is an alternative name for the Thames, applied in general only as it flows past Oxford. It has no clear historical or geographical derivation, seeming to be merely an Oxford affectation. Carroll himself remains neutral on the matter, always referring simply to 'the river'.

† The rooms in question would have pre-dated the Meadow Buildings which comprise the current southern façade of the college, and were completed in 1865.

for 40 years. All the walks on Ch. Ch. meadow covered.' *Jackson's Oxford Journal* of 30 March 1867 was slightly more restrained, reporting that 'the floods in this neighbourhood during the earlier part of the week have been higher than any experienced since November 1852' and that 'the whole of the low-lying lands were between three and four feet submerged' and 'Christ Church Meadow Walks were similarly flooded'. Spectators on Magdalen Bridge 'saw a vast fresh-water lake, the wind lashing its waters into fury. Several sheep and lambs are reported to have been seen in the water at this point.' Alice's 'plaintive tone' when saying 'Things flow about so here!' surely echoed the laments of many a flood-affected Oxford resident of the time!

∾ TEXT ∾

Alice enters the Shop in 'Wool and Water' after following the White Queen across one of the little brooks which represent the horizontal edges of the squares on the chessboard (hedges being the vertical edges). The Queen transmogrifies into the Sheep, who is behind the counter, and, somewhat creepily, she is busy knitting.

> 'Can you row?' the Sheep asked, handing her a pair of knitting-needles as she spoke.
> 'Yes, a little – but not on land – and not with needles –' Alice was beginning to say, when suddenly the needles turned into oars in her hands, and she found they were in a little boat, gliding along between banks: so there was nothing for it but to do her best.
> 'Feather!' cried the Sheep, as she took up another pair of needles.

The Sheep repeats the word several more times.*

---

* In rowing, the feathering of oars is to turn the blades horizontal at the end of each pull, and move them forward again for the next pull by skimming the surface. Alice: 'I can remember what hard work it was rowing upstream from Nuneham but this was nothing if we thought we were learning and getting on. It was a proud day when we could "feather our oars" properly.' (*Cornhill Magazine*, July 1932, p8.)

19. 'The Inundation of Christchurch Meadows, Oxford' from the *Illustrated London News* of 4 December 1852 (at the end of Carroll's second year at Oxford). The central spire is Tom Tower, which marks the entrance to Christ Church from St Aldate's. The view seems likely to have been taken from Grandpont House.

'*Why* do you say "Feather" so often?' Alice asked at last, rather vexed. 'I'm not a bird!'

'You are,' said the Sheep: 'you're a little goose.'

This offended Alice a little, so there was no more conversation for a minute or two, while the boat glided gently on, sometimes among beds of weeds (which made the oars stick fast in the water, worse than ever), and sometimes under trees, but always with the same tall river-banks frowning over their heads.

Later Alice spies some scented rushes.

'Please may we wait and pick some?' Alice pleaded. 'If you don't mind stopping the boat for a minute.'

'How am *I* to stop it?' said the Sheep. 'If you leave off rowing, it'll stop of itself.'

So the boat was left to drift down the stream as it would, till it glided gently in among the waving rushes. And then the little sleeves were carefully rolled up, and the little arms were plunged in elbow-deep, to get hold of the rushes a good long way down before breaking them off – and for a while Alice forgot all about the Sheep and the knitting, as she bent over the side of the boat, with just the ends of her tangled hair dipping into the water – while with bright eager eyes she caught at one bunch after another of the darling scented rushes.

'Wool and Water' ends back at the Shop. After a play on the word 'crab', another rowing term, the Sheep asks Alice if it is a crab that she wishes to buy. Put on the spot, she decides that it is an egg that she wants, which leads to the next chapter, called 'Humpty Dumpty'. Alice's departure from 'the very queerest shop I ever saw' is by means of crossing another little brook at the far end of the shop to reach the next row of the chessboard.

7

TRILL MILL STREAM

When composing the preceding passage from 'Wool and Water', Carroll could have had in mind almost any of Oxford's myriad streams. Yet the one that flows closest to Alice's Shop, the Trill Mill Stream, is an unlikely candidate – even though in real life it would certainly have been a contributory factor in any local flooding. Despite its attractive name, the Trill Mill Stream was not at this time the sort of waterway that would have tempted a young girl to plunge in her little arms or dip her tangled hair. The reason was the Stream's notorious reputation for pollution.

Alice's son, Caryl Hargreaves, alludes to this in his introduction to Alice's recollections in *Cornhill Magazine*. Inviting the reader to accompany the three girls from Christ Church to Folly Bridge (see page 41), Hargreaves wrote that 'the way down to the river and to the boats was alongside the Till [sic] Mill stream, an evil-smelling and altogether undesirable approach to the river'.

Indeed it was! The notoriety of the Trill Mill Stream's polluted waters stretched back centuries. In 1293 a royal decree ordered that 'the Bakers and Brewers of Oxford should not make use of the corrupt water of the Trillmill stream', yet in the latter years of the seventeenth century the Oxford diarist and historian Anthony Wood bemoaned that its waters were still being used to make 'very unwholesome liquor; which without doubt is the author of several diseases among us'.*

By the nineteenth century, the polluted watercourse had acquired the ironic, erudite nickname 'Pactolus', derived from the stream of that name in the Greek myth of King Midas, whose touch turned everything

---

* Anthony Wood, *History and Antiquities of the University of Oxford* I. (John Gutch, 1792) p345.

into gold. In *Curiosities of Natural History*, Francis Buckland quipped in 1859 that 'the modern Pactolus does not contain gold but something convertible into gold, if used by the farmer as manure'. W. E. Sherwood described it as 'a filthy ditch, generally known as Pactolus, as it was black with half the sewage of Oxford'.* A Christ Church plan of 1848 labels the stream Pactolus, but the earliest reference found comes, rather surprisingly, from the direction of the Oxford City Corporation, in a drainage report of 1833.

To tackle the problem, the stream was culverted in 1863, causing it to flow underground near Oxford Castle and to re-emerge in Christ Church's grounds (now comprising the Memorial Gardens, which were laid out in 1926 – see Appendix 2).† Evidently the impact was not immediate. In the September 1871 issue of the short-lived Oxford journal *Dark Blue*, the stream was decried as one 'whose bottom contains ten feet of seething odour, the surface of which is so vile, that it does but disgust, defile and infect a whole population'. The problem was not confined to the Trill Mill Stream, however. The article continues:

> Nasty, very nasty, is every branch of the Cherwell, dead-doggy and befouled is Isis, venomous is Pactolus; crawling with insect life is the railway-cutting pond which supplies Oxford with water, but the gas works, in respect of stink, are – simply — .

No words, evidently, were adequate – or at least, none fit for Victorian sensibilities! One can understand why Dean Liddell approved the new, wide, tree-lined avenue still apparent today. Leading directly from the college to the Thames, and 'superseding the narrow, damp, and unsavoury path' alongside the Trill Mill Stream, it was formally opened in 1872 by Princess Louise. To mark the occasion, 'the crews of the Eights assembled in the Deanery Garden, and walked in procession from the Meadow gate to the Barges, carrying the flags of their respective colleges'.‡

---

* W. E. Sherwood, *Oxford Rowing* (Frowde, Oxford, 1900) p89.
† It seems likely that Dean Liddell would have been instrumental in this measure. Drainage was a particular concern of his, and 'when Sir Henry Acland brought to Christ Church a learned German professor who was very anxious to have a sight of the famous writer of the Lexicon … they were told that he was in Christ Church Meadow.' Finding no sign of Liddell there, they were eventually informed that 'he has just gone down the drain'. (Thompson, p196.)
‡ Thompson, p165.

8

CHRIST CHURCH MEADOW

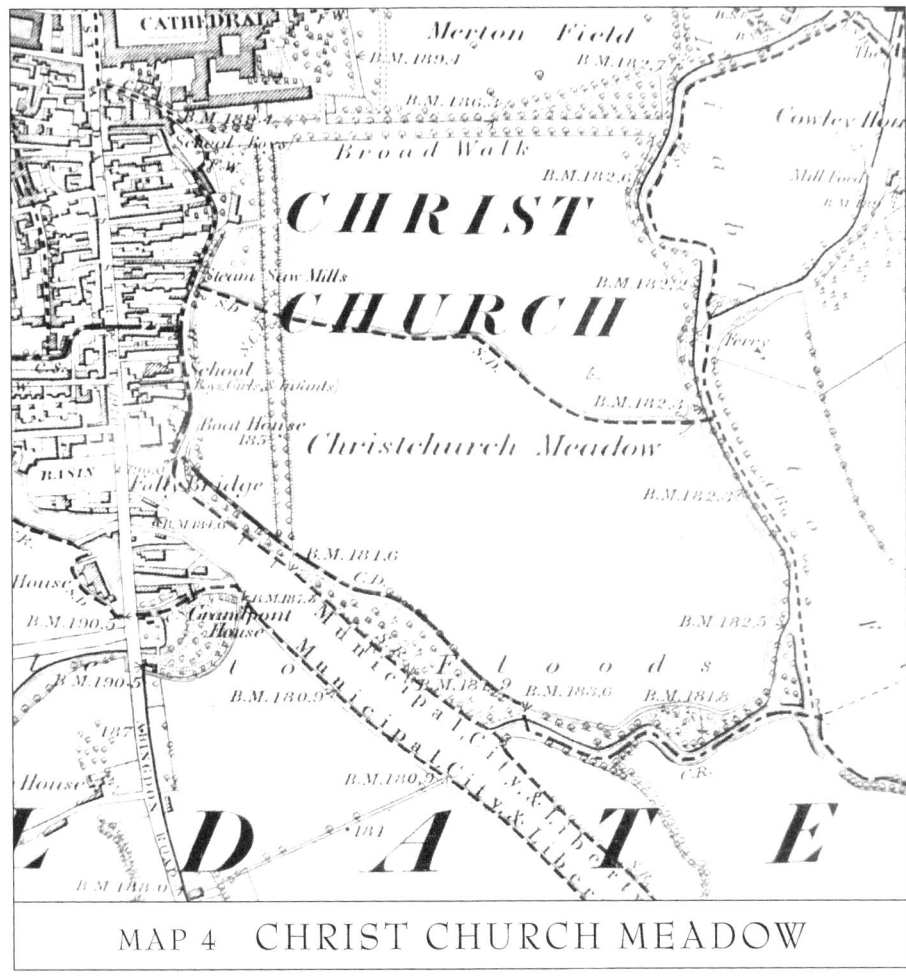

MAP 4 CHRIST CHURCH MEADOW

Extract of Ordnance Survey 6-inch-to-a-mile of 1876. Christ Church and its Cathedral are top left; the new tree-lined avenue from the college down to the river is clearly shown, and towards the bottom left is Grandpont House, spanning a sidestream which defined the city boundary. The River Cherwell marks the eastern extent of the Meadow. In 1884 its most easterly branch would be realigned to flow more directly into the Thames as a flood-prevention measure.

25 FEB. 1856

First afternoon of the torpids. Frank and I went down to see them and fell in with the Liddell party. (Mrs. L., her sister, and the two eldest children). We bumped University, and are now second. *

6 MARCH 1856

Made friends with little Harry Liddell, (whom I first spoke to down at the boats last week): he is certainly the handsomest boy I ever saw.

25 APRIL 1856 (Fri.)

Went over with Southey† in the afternoon to the Deanery, to try and take a photograph of the Cathedral: both attempts proved failures. The three little girls were in the garden most of the time, and we became excellent friends: we tried to group them in the foreground of the picture, but they were not patient sitters. I mark this day with a white stone.

22 OCT. 1856

Fell in with Harry and Ina Liddell down in the meadow, and took them up to see my book of photographs.

---

* This day marked Carroll's first meeting with Dean Liddell's immediate family, but he had already encountered some distant cousins by chance the previous year, in Whitburn (South Tyne). For an explanation of 'bumping' see page 79. Frank was Carroll's cousin, also a Christ Church scholar, Francis Hume Dodgson (1834–1917), oldest son of Carroll's uncle Hassard.

† Dr Reginald Southey (1835–99), a Christ Church graduate who encouraged Carroll's interest in photography. At the time Ina was nearly seven, Alice nearly four, and Edith two. Carroll took delivery of his own first camera on 1 May 1856. An intriguing character in the 1850s novel *Verdant Green* is Fanny Bouncer, described as 'a clever proficient in the fascinating art of photography', and capable both of taking the photographs and producing calotypes using her own chemicals – much as Carroll did, using the wet collodion method.

3 NOV. 1856 *(Mon.)*

Met Miss Prickett, the governess, at the Deanery, walking with Ina, and settled that I would come over on Wednesday morning, if it is fine. I also asked her to try and secure some of the Aclands* coming over to be taken: there are five or six of them, and Southey says they are a beautiful family.

5 NOV. 1856 *(Wed.)*

The morning was fair, and I took my camera over to the Deanery, just in time to see the whole party (except Edith) set off with the carriage and ponies, a disappointment for me, as it is the last vacant morning I shall have in the term. However, I must manage to clear another morning.

10 NOV. 1856

Went to the Deanery to take portraits at two, but the light failed, and I only got one of Harry. I spent an hour or so afterwards with the children and governess, up in the schoolroom, making them paper boats etc.

5 FEB. 1857

Walking in the afternoon I fell in with Ina Liddell and the governess, and returned with them to the Deanery, where I spent about an hour with the young party in the schoolroom.

22 FEB. 1857 *(Sun.)*

Met (as usual) Harry and Ina in the meadow, and took Harry with me into chapel.

---

* Carroll photographed several of the Acland children soon after, including Sarah (1849–1930), who went on to become a notable pioneer of colour photography.

2 APRIL 1857

Harry came over for his arithmetic lesson in the morning, and in the afternoon I joined and walked with him, Ina, and the governess.

12 APRIL 1857 (Sun.)

In the afternoon I walked in the meadow (as usual) with Harry, Ina, and the governess, and took Harry to chapel. This last I do not mean to do again for some time, as he becomes less and less attentive on each occasion.

17 MAY 1857

Took Harry Liddell to chapel, and afterwards walked back with the children to the Deanery. I find to my great surprise that my notice of them is construed by some men into attentions to the governess, Miss Prickett.

It would be inconsiderate to the governess to give any further occasion for remarks of the sort. For this reason I shall avoid taking any public notice of the children in future.*

27 MAY 1857 (Wed.)

Met Ina and the governess in the morning and settled that if possible Southey and I would come over on Friday to take portraits. Took Harry down to see the races in the evening. We went on to the barge for a short time, but I did not like staying long, as some of the men there were very undesirable acquaintances for him.

---

* It was a resolve which lasted all of ten days.

2 JUNE 1857

Spent the morning at the Deanery... Harry was away, but the two dear little girls, Ina and Alice, were with me all morning. To try the lens, I took a picture of myself, for which Ina took off the cap, and of course considered it all her own doing!

I mark this day with a white stone.

2 AUG. 1862 (Sat.)

Mrs. Brodie brought her children over to be photographed in the morning ... after which Margaret and Ida* came down again to go, with the Liddells, Harcourt, and myself, on the water. Then back to croquêt at the Deanery, and Harcourt and I went there again after dinner to escort the Brodies home, the Liddells also insisting on walking there and back with us.

13 NOV. 1862

I found Ina, Alice, and Edith in the quadrangle, and had a little talk with them, a rare event of late.

17 FEB. 1863

It seems I am destined to meet the Liddells perpetually just now. I walked in the Broad Walk with them in the morning, and in the afternoon Hoole and I went to the Ch. Ch. Athletic Sports, and fell in with them and kept with them most of the afternoon.

13 MARCH 1863

Went into the Broad Walk soon after 11, and met Alice and Edith with Miss Prickett, and had a very pleasant two hours' walking

---

* Two of the daughters, aged about 12 and 10 respectively, of the chemist Benjamin Collins Brodie (1817–80).

with them round the meadow. I began a poem the other day in which I mean to embody something about Alice (if I can at all please myself by any description of her), and which I mean to call 'Life's Pleasance'.*

20 MARCH 1863

Spent the morning, as usual, partly in Hall, and partly in the Broad Walk, where I had the company of Ina and Edith with Miss Prickett.

Took a second walk out towards Hinksey, and again fell in with the Liddells, with whom (after a race with Ina on the bridge over the reservoir) I walked back into Oxford.

22 APRIL 1863

Little Mary Norris … told me of the flower-show going on in the new Exchange. I went in, and there fell in with Ina, Edith, and Miss Prickett (and also Lady Brodie and her five).† I afterwards had a very pleasant walk with them round by the two Hinkseys, going up on to the hill near Ferry Hinksey.

27 APRIL 1863

Walked towards Hinksey and fell in with Ina, Edith and governess, and went with them to our old cricket-ground, to see the militia drilled.

29 APRIL 1863

There is no variety in my life to record just now except meetings

---

* The origins, presumably, of the acrostic verse at the end of *Through the Looking-Glass* (see page 14).
† Note that Philothea Brodie has become 'Lady' since the previous mention of her in 1862, her husband having succeeded to the title on the death that year of his father Sir Benjamin Collins Brodie, surgeon to Queen Victoria. Mary Norris was the daughter of the President of Corpus Christi College. The new Corn Exchange was inside the old Town Hall (rebuilt in 1897).

with the Liddells, the record of which has become almost continuous. I walked with them in the meadow this morning.

22 MAY 1863

Walked on the Abingdon road, returning by Hinksey, and overtook the Liddells on my way back, and took them back again almost to Hinksey. They gave me an account of the outrage in the Deanery garden last night. The whole of the flowers and shrubs have been destroyed – perpetrators unknown.

17 JUNE 1863

The children left the Bazaar at 4 to play croquêt with the Royal guests. Escorted the Haringtons down to the boat procession, and also back, when I had a long argument with the driver, who wanted double pay.*

6 MAY 1864

Walked on the other side of the river, and met Ina, Alice and Edith, with Miss Prickett: we inspected the new 'grand stand' intended for spectators of the boat-races. Went down to the races, and saw Ch. Ch. bump Magdalen.

18 MAY 1867

Paid a visit to Mrs. Liddell, and had a long chat with her walking about the Deanery garden, a thing I have not done for years. She sent me some numbers of a magazine ... to send to my sisters, to which Ina added a paper.

---

* The bazaar in aid of the Radcliffe Infirmary was held at St John's College as part of the Commemoration Week celebrations which were made especially noteworthy by the presence of the Prince and Princess of Wales. So Alice played croquêt against royalty on this day, much as the fictional Alice did in *Wonderland*! Richard Harington (1835–1911) was a former pupil of Carroll's at Christ Church. Carroll took many photographs of his daughters, Beatrice (1852–1936) and (Alice) Margaret (1854–1901).

CHRIST CHURCH MEADOW

In contrast to the path alongside the fetid waters of the Trill Mill Stream, Christ Church Meadow itself, of which the Stream marks its western extent, has always been a supremely attractive place to take walks. Carroll's diaries have many references to walking here with the Liddell girls, apparently usually by coincidence rather than by arrangement – although their routine does seem to have been fairly predictable. Alice: 'We used always to go out for about an hour's walk before luncheon at one o'clock. Sometimes we went out towards Bagley Wood, sometimes round Christ Church meadow, sometimes towards North Oxford, which was then open fields.'* Mary Prickett, the governess, would of course always accompany them.

Occasionally Carroll mentions more distant encounters, notably out towards the villages of North (or Ferry) and South Hinksey. Inevitably these walks would mean crossing the many small streams derived from the braiding of the Thames on the Berkshire (western) side of its main course (see Map 3). It is noticeable that almost the only local walks of which Carroll makes any mention in the creatively important years of 1862–64 are those with the Liddells, even though, as an avid walker all his life, he no doubt went on many, many more. He seems glumly aware of this pattern, writing on 29 April 1863: 'There is no variety in my life to record just now except meetings with the Liddells.'

Another of Alice's regular walking companions was canine. A 'special pleasure was to be allowed to take Rover out for a walk. Rover was a retriever belonging to a well-known Oxford tailor, called Randall, who lived in a house built on arches over the Isis, which he christened Grandpont'.† This extraordinary house (the name deriving from the

---

* *Cornhill Magazine*, July 1932, p4. Bagley Wood lies a few miles south west of Oxford.
† *Cornhill Magazine*, July 1932, p4.

20. Grandpont House, with its 'ingenious system of small rivers' instead of cellars. The home of Alderman Thomas Randall (and his dog Rover!) when Alice Liddell was a girl, photographed by Henry Taunt (1900). (*Oxfordshire History Centre*)

original Norman name for Folly Bridge) was built in 1785. It is mentioned in *The Adventures of Mr. Verdant Green* as 'that eccentric mansion … possessing in the place of cellars an ingenious system of small rivers to thoroughly irrigate its foundations'. Randall is also referenced by name in the novel. Indeed, he was among Oxford's best known tradesmen on account of his prominent High Street premises, his role as a councillor and alderman, and his superior education, and although he was indeed a tailor, he preferred to be thought of as a hatter. Aha! For more about this intriguing individual please see Appendix 3.

On the subject of clothing: 'Mr. Dodgson always wore black clergyman's clothes in Oxford, but, when he took us out on the river, he used to wear white flannel trousers. He also replaced his black top-hat by a hard white straw hat on these occasions, but of course retained his black boots, because in those days white tennis shoes had never been heard of. He always carried himself upright, almost more than upright, as if he had swallowed a poker.'*

From the 1840s onwards, Christ Church Meadow's bank was lined with imposing, ornate barges belonging to various colleges (see Appendix 4). These vessels had a dual purpose: to provide somewhere for rowers to change and for spectators to view the regular races held on this stretch of the river. The scene in about 1857 is described by the Halls in *The Book of the Thames*. Of the Exeter College and newly purchased University Boat Club barges they wrote:

> Both are of costly workmanship, the latter being somewhat sombre in style when we saw it, but now, as we learn, richly decorated with colour, and displaying the armorial bearings of all the colleges: the former still flaunting in scarlet and gold, although age and use have somewhat tarnished its brilliancy. These 'vessels' serve as floating club-houses, and are well supplied with newspapers, periodicals, and writing materials, and have dressing-rooms for members. They are not calculated for making voyages, and are rarely released from their moorings.

Cuthbert Bede's fictional hero Verdant Green frequented 'the floating reading-room of the University barge' in the early 1850s. There he could study the news of the day, and

> look out upon the picturesque river with its moving life of eights and four-oars sweeping past with measured stroke. A great feature of the river picture, just about this time, was the crowd of newly introduced canoes; their occupants, in every variety of bright-coloured shirts and caps, flashing up and down a double paddle, the ends of which were painted in gay colours, or emblazoned with the owner's crest.

The novel also includes a description of the view across Christ Church Meadow:

---

* *Cornhill Magazine*, July 1932, p9.

Through openings in the trees there were glimpses of grey old college-buildings; then came the walk along the banks, the Isis shining like molten silver, and fringed around with barges and boats; then another stretch of green meadows; then a cloud of steam from the railway-station; and a background of gently rising hills.[*]

It was at the three main rowing events of the academic year that the college barges really came into their own. The Torpid races were held early in the year, for the second-string crews. The major event, then and now, was Eights' Week, held in May, and so called because the crews consist of eight rowers. Inter-college rivalry was fierce, and the races always attracted a great number of spectators: townspeople as well as students. Nineteenth-century Oxford novelists were fond of including Eights' Week or the other major river event of the summer – the 'procession of boats' during Commemoration Week – in their plots. This was not just because of the descriptive opportunity offered by the excitement and colour of the day, but because the occasion enabled writers to introduce some romance into the storyline, with the arrival of female relatives in a city with a disproportionally large male population.

In *Tom Brown at Oxford*, Thomas Hughes[†] describes the procession of boats during a Commemoration Week of the early 1840s:

> The barges above and below the University barge, which occupied the post of honour, were also covered with ladies, and Christchurch Meadow swarmed with gay dresses and caps and gowns. On the opposite side the bank was lined with a crowd in holiday clothes, and the punts plied across without intermission loaded with people, until the groups stretched away down the towing path in an almost continuous line to the starting place. Then one after another the racing-boats, all painted and polished

---

[*] The station referred to is Oxford's first, opened by the Great Western Railway Co. in 1844, on the south side of the Thames near Folly Bridge. It was superseded by a new station, near Oxford's current station, in October 1852.

[†] Thomas Hughes (1822–96) was at Oxford in the early 1840s, and was an excellent oarsman. His brother George was still more proficient, and rowed in a famous inter-varsity race against Cambridge in 1843 which is said to have marked the elevation of the sport to *the* predominant University recreation (see Appendix 3). Both Hughes brothers attended Rugby School (the setting for *Tom Brown's Schooldays*) a few years prior to Carroll, who was a pupil there between 1846 and 1849. Another Rugby old boy was Matthew Arnold (1822–88), who penned the famous 'dreaming spires' description of Oxford in his 1867 poem *Thyrsis*.

21. 'The Oxford Commemoration: the Procession of Boats' (*Illustrated London News*, 27 June 1863). The Trinity College boat, as 'Head of the River', is positioned in front of the University barge (middle right), from which the Prince and Princess of Wales watched the proceedings. The crew hold their oars aloft, reciprocating the salute of each boat as it passes in the direction of Folly Bridge (in the distance).

up for the occasion, with the college flags drooping at their sterns, put out and passed down to their stations, and the bands played, and the sun shone his best.

In *Verdant Green* the influx of femininity is stressed rather more: 'How a few flounces and bright girlish smiles can change the aspect of the sternest homes of knowledge! How sunlight can be brought into the gloomiest nooks of learning by the beams that irradiate happy girlish faces.'

It is rare to find a hero of a nineteenth-century Oxford novel who was not in some way responsible for a triumph by his college's boating crew. Carroll, although he enjoyed rowing for pleasure, seems not to have been especially interested in these competitive events. Certainly there are few references to them in his diaries. However, the racing did provide him with his first opportunity for social interaction with the Liddell family, when the Torpid races of February 1856 provided an opportunity to talk to Alice's mother, Lorina Hannah née Reeve (1826–1910); Lorina's sister, Mrs Pleasance Elizabeth Fellows (1823–1898); and the two eldest children, Harry (1847–1911) and Ina (1849–1930).

In June 1863 Carroll was one of an especially large number of spectators at the Commemoration Week procession of boats, made notable by the presence of the recently married Prince and Princess of Wales. The Prince had previously attended Christ Church as a student for two years, and the visit was arranged in order for him to receive an honorary degree. It was an occasion which enthralled the entire city, both Town and Gown (that is, both the inhabitants of Oxford and the members of its University). *Jackson's Oxford Journal* was effusive, devoting nearly half of its entire news output of 20 June 1863 to the event: 'Never before was the old City so full of noble and distinguished visitors, never was College hospitality dispensed on a larger scale, and never were festivities more exciting or more brilliant.' The Prince and Princess were guests of the Liddells at Christ Church. Their first public engagement on arriving on Tuesday 16 June was to award prizes to members of the University Rifle Corps, whose competition on Port Meadow the previous week had been witnessed by Carroll. The next day, Wednesday 17 June, the Prince and Princess played croquêt with the Liddell girls in the afternoon – how interesting, considering that the Alice of Wonderland also played croquêt against royalty! – and then attended the traditional Commemoration Week procession of boats. *Jackson's* reported that a

> grand stand had been erected on the Berkshire side of the river to accommodate upwards of a thousand members and friends of the University Boat Club, both banks of the Isis were thronged with spectators; barges and rafts were eagerly scrambled for, and numberless boats of every description speckled the water.

The royal couple left the Deanery about 6pm, and at Folly Bridge 'embarked in a very handsome boat, stylishly fitted up, built expressly for the occasion by Messrs. Salter, by order of the University Boat Club'. In this vessel the royal couple were rowed as far as the confluence with the Cherwell, then back to take pride of place on the University barge. Then came the procession, described in the *Illustrated London News* of 27 June: as 'Head of the River', the Trinity College boat, came

> flying over the water as silently and quickly as a bird, [and] stopped in its own length before the Royal barge, that the boats of all the other colleges might do homage to their supremacy and past year's triumph over them. This they did in the usual manner as they came by in long procession, tossing their oars in honour of Trinity, and then waving their hats and cheering in honour of the Princess, who seemed deeply amused and interested in the whole proceeding.

Then 'the whole long file of boats swept under Folly Bridge, and, turning there, came back again in procession two and two abreast'. Evidently, it was common during the Commemoration procession for some kind of mishap to occur, and if it did not, one was contrived, for the amusement of the spectators. Consequently, Balliol's Torpid crew's boat obligingly turned over immediately in front of the Prince and Princess. In addition, according to *Jackson's*, 'there were several other duckings, which excited great merriment, and one of the rafts, through unequal weight on one end, was partially capsized, with some effect on the nerves of the female portion of its crew'.

The next afternoon, Thursday 18 June, the royal couple departed by train, and 'having taken a cordial leave of the Dean, Mrs. Liddell, and their children, the special train moved off, amidst hearty cheers'. *Jackson's* concluded: 'And thus ended a Commemoration the like of which Oxford has never seen before and which none, of this generation at least, can expect to see again.'

Published two years earlier, *Tom Brown at Oxford* includes a very similar scene. Having triumphed as 'Head of the River' in the May Eights, the fictional St Ambrose College boat, of which Tom is a crew member, is stationed (as Trinity's really was in 1863) to receive the acknowledgements of the other 23 eight-oars in the procession, 'with their flags flying, and all the crews in uniform'. Then 'the boats passed up one by one; and, as each came opposite to the St. Ambrose boat, the crews tossed their oars and cheered, and the St. Ambrose crew tossed their oars and cheered in return, and the whole ceremony went off in triumph.' However, one of the Torpids – boats which contain 'the refuse of the rowing men – generally awkward or very young oarsmen' – fares less well. The boat, 'having sustained her crew gallantly to the saluting point, and allowed them to get their oars fairly in the air, proceeded gravely to turn over on her side, and shoot them out into the stream'.

Christ Church Meadow is bordered by rivers on three sides. Before we venture a short distance along the third of these, the River Cherwell, the other, northernmost, boundary deserves notice, if only on account of its intriguing modern name of Deadman's Walk. The popular explanation is that the path, which runs just outside the old city walls, was once the funeral route for Jewish burials conducted on part of what is now the Botanic Garden. Another possible explanation, however, stems from two early Oxford guidebooks, and is supported, conveniently enough, by one of the Liddell sisters' closest childhood friends.

The earliest known reference is in the *Gentleman and Lady's Pocket Companion for Oxford* (1747): 'Dead Man's Walk, intimating, I presume, that it will almost restore a Dead man to life', with the rationale for that idea coming two years later: 'The Dead Man's Walk, being the warmest Winter Walk in Europe'.[*]

The belief in the salutary effects of the location were still apparent a century later, espoused by Henry Acland (1815–1900), the Liddells' own doctor. In her unpublished memoir, Acland's daughter Sarah (1849–1930), recalling the 1850s, wrote: 'I well remember I first saw the Liddell children as they were being sunned in the Deadman's Walk, as we were by our Nurse.' She also made this claim: 'One other Ch. Ch. memory of those early days was that of going down the river with the Liddells taken by Mr. Dodgson (Lewis Carroll) who used to tell us stories, bits of which became Alice in Wonderland.'[†] As Carroll makes no mention of these trips in his surviving diaries, they presumably occurred between 1858 and 1862. The Acland family continued to be a familiar sight on the river:

> Dr. Acland was fond of the sea. As he lived so far away from it he consoled himself by the creation of what he called "The Acland Eight". Mrs. Acland would steer the boat, her husband was stroke, and the sons would take the oars in order of seniority. During the summer this crew would make its stately way up and down the river.[‡]

Henry Acland seems to have taken over Carroll's earlier role as an organiser of river trips for the Liddell girls: in 1869, for instance, he and his son Harry 'rowed Alice and Edith down the Thames to Sandford on the first summer evening'.[§]

---

[*] John Pointer, *Oxoniensis Academia* (1749) p76.
[†] 'Memories in my 81st Year' (Bodleian: Ms Eng. Misc. d.214), p15 & p17. Carroll makes no specific mention of Deadman's Walk in his diaries but his friend Thomas Vere Bayne did, on 27 December 1887, for instance (when afflicted with gout): 'Sunny but colder. Venture along the Dead Man's Wall, but my foot is certainly no better, rather more painful.' (Christ Church MS536.)
[‡] Sheila Birkenhead, *Against Oblivion: the Life of Joseph Severn* (1943) p221.
[§] Giles Hudson, *Sarah Angelina Acland: first lady of colour photography* (2012) p8.

9

RIVER
CHERWELL

22. 'A Punting Scene by the Christ Church Meadows Oxford' from *College Life* by Edward Bradley (c1850). Tom Tower and Christ Church Cathedral are in the background.

3 MARCH 1857

Went on the river with Skeffington and Wilfred. * *We went about 5 miles up the Cherwell, just after clearing the rapids the bow-oar broke, and we turned homewards, after binding up the fracture with the painter in the best way we could.*

18 APRIL 1857

Went up the Cherwell in a gig with Joyce (Senior) [†] *and Harry Liddell.*

10 MARCH 1863

Edwin [‡] *and I went into the Broad Walk to see the three Deanery children plant three trees along the Cherwell, in memory of the day, each delivered a short speech over her tree 'long life to this tree, and may it prosper from this auspicious day', and they named them Alexandra, Albert, and Victoria. After the tree-planting we escorted the Liddells and Mrs. Reeve* [§] *to see the ox roasted whole near Worcester,* [¶] *which was <u>not</u> an exciting spectacle. At three was the last Torpid race, for which we went on to the barge, and of course met the Liddells again. After Hall we went to the Deanery for the children, and set out. We soon lost the others, and Alice and I with Edwin, took the round of*

---

* Carroll's brothers Skeffington Dodgson (1836–1919) and Wilfred Dodgson (1838–1914), both of whom were studying at Christ Church.
† Probably Francis Hayward Joyce (1829–1906), Christ Church Student and tutor.
‡ Carroll's youngest brother Edwin Dodgson (1846–1913), who was still at school at Rugby at this time.
§ Mrs Lorina Reeve, née Farr (1794–1879), Alice's grandmother from Suffolk.
¶ Meaning Worcester College, nicknamed 'Botany Bay' in *The Adventures of Mr. Verdant Green* on account of its remoteness from all the other colleges. The ox-roast was actually in Jericho (*Jackson's Oxford Journal*, 14 March 1863), which lies immediately to the north of Worcester College.

all the principal streets in about two hours, bringing her home by half-past nine. The mob was dense, but well conducted. The fireworks abundant, and some of the illuminations very beautiful. It was delightful to see the thorough abandonment with which Alice enjoyed the whole thing.* The Wedding-day of the Prince of Wales I mark with a white stone.

23. A doodle by Henry Liddell: 'As chairman of the new governing body of Christ Church, he whiled away the interminable meetings by taking out his gold pen, wiping it carefully on his sleeve and drawing on his blotter.' (Gordon, p99) (*Governing Body of Christ Church, Oxford*)

---

* The evening was one which was still etched in Alice's memory almost 70 years later. 'The crowd in the streets was very great, and I clung tightly to the hand of the strong man on either side of me. The colleges were all lit up, and the High Street was a mass of illuminations of all sorts and kinds.' (*Cornhill Magazine*, July 1932, p9.)

24. 'Magdalen Tower and Bridge, from the Cherwell', from the 1855 University Almanac (W. Radcliffe after Peter de Wint).

RIVER CHERWELL

Almost all of the rowing trips recorded by Carroll were on the Thames. Only two outings on its tributary, the River Cherwell, are known, both in 1857 (one of them with Harry Liddell). At the time, the Cherwell had only one navigable confluence with the Thames, flowing, as today, immediately alongside Christ Church Meadow (see Map 4). A second, more direct, outlet to the Thames was created in 1884, as a flood-prevention measure. The scheme was first proposed by 1882 by Sir John Hawkshaw, and included the complete removal of Iffley Lock. It had the wholehearted backing of Dean Liddell and Benjamin Jowett, then the Vice-Chancellor of the University, who jointly pledged the £14,000 needed. In the end, only the new branch of the Cherwell, initially known as the 'Vice-Chancellor's Cut', was achieved.* This helped to re-define both the island now occupied by the boathouses (which replaced the picturesque college barges from 1939 onwards) and the much larger Aston's Eyot† downstream.

Carroll's only other mention of the Cherwell came on Tuesday 10 March 1863. This was the day that the Prince of Wales (later King Edward VII) married Princess Alexandra of Denmark. Carroll took a stroll along the Broad Walk that day, and came across the three Liddell girls planting saplings on the bank of the Cherwell in honour of the day. Later on that day, Carroll joined the Liddells on the Christ Church barge to watch the Torpids, and in the evening he and his brother Edwin took Alice through the crowded streets of Oxford to see the celebratory illuminations and fireworks.

---

* Thompson, p197.
† The word 'eyot' derives from the Old English for a small island, especially in a river. The 'ey' ending of so many place names bordering the river in Oxford – Medley, Binsey, Osney, Hinksey, and even 'Portmanheit' (the original name of Port Meadow) – demonstrates the 'waterland' nature of the city's western fringes.

25. The confluence of the Rivers Thames and Cherwell, from Mr & Mrs S. C. Hall's *The Book of the Thames* (1859).

26. A busy boating scene a short distance above Iffley Lock, from *The Adventures of Mr. Verdant Green* (1853). The eponymous hero is in the 'The Sylph', centre front.

IFFLEY
LOCK

27. 'Starting the Favorite' [sic] from *Reminiscences of Oxford Varsity Life* (anon), showing a rowing eight at the start above Iffley Lock. The date is not certain, but the publishers (T. & G. Shrimpton, Oxford) traded by this name from before 1852 until 1871. Morrell's Brewery was Oxford's longest lasting, closing in 1998. The advertised 'Entire' was a popular, strong beer similar to porter.

26 MAY 1862

Went down the river with Southey, taking Ina, Alice, and Edith with us: we only went to Iffley. Even then it was hard work rowing up again, the stream is so strong.* Afterwards we went in and had a game of croquêt with them in the Deanery garden.

30 JUNE 1862

Went with Atkinson to the boat procession: then he sculled me down to Iffley: then to the fireworks in Holywell Green. (On Saturday we went to Blondin's 'low rope' performance, and met the Liddells there).†

17 APRIL 1863

Harry Liddell came to ask me to go with them down the river. Miss Prickett came (by Mrs. Liddell's wish) with them. (I quite think that Ina is now so tall as to look odd without an escort.) I got Walter Scott to come and help to row, but he proved almost of no use. Harry sculled by himself, managed to be always in the way, and generally rather spoiled what would otherwise have been a very pleasant expedition.‡

---

* This was Alice's first identifiable river trip. In *Three Men in a Boat* (1889), Jerome K. Jerome was of the opinion that 'between Iffley and Oxford is the most difficult bit of the river I know… First the current drives you onto the right bank, and then on to the left, then it takes you out into the middle, turns you round three times, and carries you upstream again, and always ends by trying to smash you up against a college barge.'

† Charles Blondin (1824–97) was the stage name of the French 'hero of Niagara' who had crossed the Falls by tightrope in 1859.

‡ Walter Folliott Scott (1844–?), a Christ Church undergraduate, related to Sir Walter Scott, the author.

5 MAY 1863

Walked in the afternoon with the trio and governess by the river side to a little below Iffley.

25 MAY 1863

Fell in with the children by the Botanical Gardens, and walked with them, a very merry party, round by Iffley.*

26 MAY 1863

There is great alarm about the baby at the Deanery, and the Dean was summoned out of morning chapel to baptise it. I met the children in the meadow in the morning, and their account gave no hope for the little one.† We walked round the meadow, grave and nearly silent, a great contrast to yesterday's walk. I offered to take them on the river in the afternoon, as a change from the dullness of a sick house. We went (the three, Miss Prickett and myself) a little below the island.

26 MAY 1875

Paid my first (possibly my only) visit to Wykeham House. We were six at luncheon… I found myself treated as senior guest, and had to sit next to the young host, who was particularly unassuming and genial in manner; I do not wonder at his being so universal a favourite.‡

---

* Mentions of the Botanic Garden by Carroll are rare, yet he probably visited often: two noteworthy occasions, in 1888 and 1889, are summarised in *The Story of Lewis Carroll* by Isa Bowman (1899).

† The baby, Albert Edward Arthur (a name chosen by the Prince of Wales, who was a godfather), died on 28 May, being about eight weeks old.

‡ Wykeham House, No. 56 Banbury Road, was Leopold's residence during his period of study at Oxford between 1872 and 1875.

28. 'A Picnic to Nuneham: in Iffley Lock' from *The Graphic*, 3 June 1882.

IFFLEY LOCK

The first river lock downstream from Christ Church is at Iffley. This was the destination on the first outing that Alice is known to have taken on the river with Carroll, on 26 May 1862, although she had undoubtedly accompanied him on earlier, unrecorded, trips too. In her *Cornhill Magazine* article she recalled four or five trips per summer, but because Carroll's diaries for the period April 1858 to May 1862 are missing, a total of only eight can be identified.

The bank above Iffley Lock is where the annual Torpid and Eights races commence, overlooked by the Isis Tavern (now Isis Farmhouse), which was converted from a farm building in 1842. The starting order of the different college boats, one behind the other along the bank, is pre-defined by their ranking the previous year. The object is to catch, or 'bump', the boat immediately in front before it reaches the finish near Folly Bridge. If successful, the two boats' positions are reversed in the next heat, meaning that over the course of the week the faster crews move up the rankings, until on the final day the fastest crew of all is named 'Head of the River'.

Thomas Hughes, in *Tom Brown at Oxford*, described the overall scene during Eights' Week from the informed perspective of a former winning competitor.

> The banks of the river were crowded; and the punts plied rapidly backwards and forwards, carrying loads of men over to the Berkshire side. The university barge, and all the other barges, were decked with flags, and the band was playing lively airs.

> Small groups of gownsmen were scattered along the bank in Christchurch meadow, chiefly dons, who were really interested in the races, but, at this time of day, seldom liked to display enthusiasm enough to cross the water and go down to the starting-place. These sombre groups were lighted up here and there by the dresses of a few ladies, who were walking up and down, and watching the boats.

Iffley is significant among Thames locks in that it was the location of one of the first three seventeenth-century chamber locks (i.e. with two gates, as opposed to the single gate of the more common, but inefficient 'flash' locks) anywhere along the length of the whole Thames. The other two were at Sandford and near Abingdon. Carroll would have passed through Iffley on all of his recorded rowing trips down the river – to Rose Island, Sandford, and Nuneham.

Iffley is also the location of a rare indication that Alice Liddell's enthusiasm for boating lasted beyond her childhood years. Queen Victoria's youngest son, Prince Leopold (1853–1884), studied at Oxford between 1872 and 1875, albeit with long breaks.[*] Among Alice's pencilled notes for her recollections at the age of eighty is one about a boating trip to Iffley, where Alice accidentally gave the prince a black eye with her oar. Leopold wondered how he would explain this mishap to the Queen, who, thought Alice, would not have approved of such informal messing about in boats with young ladies. Anyway, Alice concluded, 'I was never ordered to be beheaded'.[†]

Alice's final comment is of course a reference to *Wonderland*'s Queen of Hearts, whose favourite expression was 'Off with his/her/their head(s)!', but may also imply some awareness of the overbearing control that Victoria tried to exert over her haemophiliac youngest son. The year of this incident is not specified, but was probably either 1875, during Leopold's last summer in Oxford, or 1876. In June 1875 he was able to remain in Oxford long enough attend the Commemoration Week events, having been frustrated at missing them the previous two years, and he came back again for the same occasion in 1876. A long account in *Jackson's Oxford Journal* (Saturday 24 June 1876) notes that Leopold stayed at Christ Church, that he attended the Commemoration Ball on Saturday

---

[*] Robinson Duckworth had been the prince's personal tutor, then governor, from 1866 until 1870. The very first lecture that Leopold attended was given by John Ruskin, and a few days later, on 30 November 1872, he dined at the Christ Church Deanery, where he told his sister Louise that he 'heard the charming Miss Liddells play & sing', adding that 'they are very pretty indeed & very nice' (Zeepvat, p107).

[†] Gordon, p172.

29. 'Iffley Mill and Church' from Alfred Rimmer's *Pleasant Spots Around Oxford* (1878).

17th (along with Robinson Duckworth,* 'who was quite recovered from the attack of fever which seized him when travelling with the Prince of Wales in India'), and that Leopold participated in the customary promenade along the Broad Walk on the Sunday, accompanied by the whole Liddell family: 'The bells of Christ Church were rung during the

---

* Carroll's diary for 16 June 1876: 'Duckworth came up to stay over Commemoration: I am giving him a bed, though I shall not be here.'

evening, and the promenaders dispersed when "Great Tom" struck the hour of nine.'*

More pertinently, on the Monday (19 June), Leopold was again in the company of all the Liddells to observe the customary procession of boats from 'the Bullingdon Barge, which was next to the University Barge, and had been specially set apart for their accommodation'.† In the evening, he attended the University Ball, and among the other attendees were Mrs and Miss Liddell (presumably Alice). One other interesting name in the long list was Mr Hargreaves, presumably Reginald (1852–1926), Alice's future husband. The ball was held at the Corn Exchange and adjacent Town Hall, the 'entire work of decoration and supplying the refreshments' having been entrusted to the wine merchants Foster & Son, that is, Charles (1809–1888), the husband of the Liddells' former governess Mary Prickett, and her stepson. A further opportunity for the prince to socialise with the Liddells occurred at the Masonic Ball held in the evening of the next day.

On the Thursday (22 June), 'Prince Leopold accompanied Mrs. Liddell and family and a select party on a trip by [sic] the river to Nuneham'. One notable absentee was Edith Liddell, who had been afflicted with a sudden illness on the 18th and died only a week later, an event made all the more tragic because she had become engaged to the heir to Nuneham, Aubrey Harcourt (1852–1904), only days before. According to Henry Liddell, Harcourt summarised the calamity as: 'Two years of patient waiting ... and four days of happiness.'‡ Prince Leopold was one of the pall-bearers at her funeral at Christ Church, where she was buried.

---

* 9pm was the time of curfew, when students had to return to college, although the actual time would have been (and continues to be) 9.05pm, on account of Christ Church's determined adherence to 'Oxford time' rather than that of Greenwich (which was adopted in 1852).
† Leopold had been a non-playing member of the Bullingdon Cricket Club, one of the University's first two – Magdalen was the other – although, then as now, 'cricket there was secondary to the dinners, and the men were chiefly of an expensive class'. (James Pycroft, *Oxford Memories* II. (1886) p117.)
‡ Gordon, p126.

$$\boxed{11}$$

ROSE
ISLAND

30. The Swan Inn on Rose Island (also called both Kennington and St Michael's Island) was the destination on Carroll's probable first boat outing with Ina Liddell on 5 June 1856. The photograph was taken by Henry Taunt in 1885. (*Oxfordshire History Centre*)

5 JUNE 1856

From half past four to seven, Frank and I made a boating excursion with Harry and Ina: the latter, much to my surprise, having got permission from the Dean to come. We went down to the island, and made a kind of picnic there, taking biscuits with us, and buying gingerbeer and lemonade there. Harry as before rowed stroke most of the way, and fortunately, considering the wild spirits of the children, we got home without accident, having attracted by our remarkable crew a good deal of attention from almost every one we met. Mark this day, Annalist, not only with a white stone, but as altogether dies mirabilis.*

1 MAY 1863

At half-past two Duckworth and I went down the river with the three Liddells and Miss Prickett. We did not get quite down to the island, but rowed up and down, varying the performance by songs from the children.

---

* This appears to be Ina's first outing. The 14th was on 6 August 1862 (see page 5).

ROSE ISLAND

Rose Island is on a bend in the river just below the railway bridge known as Kennington Viaduct. Work was begun on this bridge, carrying the line to the Oxfordshire town of Thame, in 1863, and was completed by the end of 1864, its progress no doubt providing a considerable additional talking-point for any river travellers at the time. The line gained later importance as a feeder for the car works at Cowley, established by William Morris, later Lord Nuffield, in 1913.

The house on Rose Island (also known historically as St Michael's Island, on account of former ownership by St Michael's parish in Oxford, and Kennington Island) was formerly a pub called The Swan Inn. This was the destination on what seems to have been the first ever river trip that Carroll made with any of the Liddell girls, on 5 June 1856. Evidently to Carroll's very great surprise (and delight, marking the day as exceptional even beyond a 'white stone' designation), he was permitted to take Ina, soon after her seventh birthday, and her brother Harry down to the island, where they bought ginger beer and lemonade, to add to the biscuits that Carroll had brought with him. Later on he would be better prepared. Alice observed:

> He always brought out with him a large basket full of cakes, and a kettle, which we used to boil under a haycock if we could find one. On rarer occasions we went out for the whole day with him, and then we took a larger basket with luncheon – cold chicken and salad and all sorts of good things.[*]

---

[*] *Cornhill Magazine*, July 1932, p7.

MAP 5

SANDFORD TO NUNEHAM

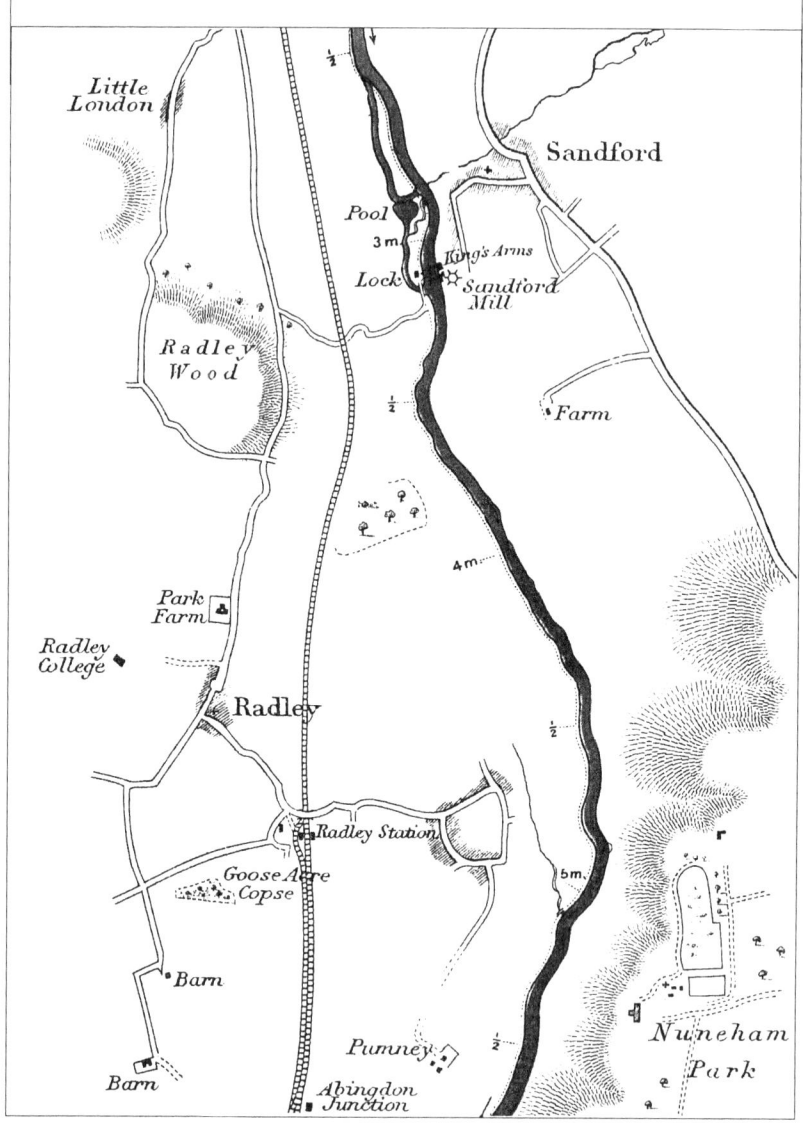

Source: Henry Taunt's *New Map of the River Thames* (ed. 3) 1879, surveyed 1878.

12

SANDFORD-ON-THAMES

31. 'Sandford Mill' from Alfred Rimmer's *Pleasant Spots Around Oxford* (1878). The King's Arms public house has retained its name to this day.

6 MARCH 1855

*Collyns, Liddon, and I went down as far as Sandford in an outriggered-gig.**

27 APRIL 1855

Down the river with Liddon, the first time this term.

3 JUNE 1856

Spent the morning at the Deanery, photographing the children. In the afternoon went with Liddon to the Horticultural Show in Worcester Gardens. Afterwards Frank and I, with Harry Liddell, went down to Sandford in a gig. We rowed with sculls down with Harry as stroke, and he steered back.

8 MAY 1857

Went down the river as far as Sandford with Frank and Harry Liddell.

26 MAY 1857

Down the river with Joyce and Harry Liddell.

24 MARCH 1858

Down the river as far as Sandford in a gig with Tyrwhitt.†

17 JUNE 1862 (Tues.)

Expedition to Nuneham. Duckworth (of Trinity) and Ina, Alice, and Edith came with us. We set out about 12½ and got

---

* John Martyn Collyns (1827–1912), graduate and later Student of Christ Church.
† Richard St John Tyrwhitt (1827–95), Student of Christ Church, artist, poet, and author.

to Nuneham about 2: dined there, then walked in the park, and set off for home about 4½. About a mile above Nuneham heavy rain came on, and after bearing it a short time I settled that we had better leave the boat and walk: three miles of this drenched us all pretty well. I went on first with the children, as they could walk much faster than Elizabeth, and took them to the only house I knew in Sandford, Mrs. Boughton's, where Ranken lodges. I left them with her to get their clothes dried, and went off to find a vehicle, but none was to be had there, so on the others arriving, Duckworth and I walked on to Iffley, whence we sent them a fly. We all had tea in my rooms about 8½, after which I took the children home, and we adjourned to Bayne's rooms for music and singing. *

13 JULY 1863

Spent this morning in the Assize Court, hearing some very petty cases, but they were interesting to me, as I have seen so little of trials. In the afternoon Kitchin† and I rowed down to the lock at Sandford and back.

---

* William Henry Ranken (1832–1920) was non-resident vicar of Sandford. Carroll preached evensong at Sandford Church on 8 June 1862, his first ever recorded sermon. The fact that Carroll specifies Duckworth's college suggests that he did not know him very well, even though he had known *of* him since 1857: on 20 May that year he attended a University Choral Society concert and noted that Duckworth sang two songs. A walk of three miles seems an exaggeration, since Nuneham and Sandford are only about two and a half miles apart along the towpath (see Map 5).

† George William Kitchin (1827–1912), a Christ Church don from 1861 to 1863. His daughter Alexandra, (1864–1925), known as Xie (pronounced 'ecksy') was Carroll's favourite photographic subject, and at the back of one of Thomas Vere Bayne's diaries is this Carrollian teaser: 'How do you attain to excellence? Take a lens and place Xie [Kitchin] in front of it.' Carroll's interest in trials at this time – he went again on 29 February 1864 – is interesting in view of the subsequent inclusion of the trial scene in *Wonderland*.

SANDFORD- ON-THAMES

The episode of 'The Pool of Tears' in *Wonderland* was inspired by what happened in Sandford on a rowing trip to Nuneham on Tuesday 17 June 1862. The party that day was an unusually large one. Carroll and the three girls were joined by Robinson Duckworth, apparently for the first time, and two of Carroll's sisters (according to Alice, although Carroll is not specific about how many of his three visitors that week – his Aunt Lucy Lutwidge, and sisters Fanny and Elizabeth – were in the boat). Soon after they had set off upstream for the journey home from Nuneham, it started to pour with rain, so they abandoned the boat and walked. Carroll went on ahead with the girls, leaving Duckworth to accompany his sisters, their pace being all the slower, no doubt, on account of the voluminous dresses of the time. One can easily imagine how 'dripping

32. Lewis Carroll's illustration of 'The Pool of Tears' from the original handwritten manuscript of 'Alice's Adventures under Ground', published in facsimile in 1886.

wet, cross, and uncomfortable' they truly were! On reaching the village of Sandford they all found shelter at the only house with which Carroll was familiar: the home of the schoolteacher, Mrs Boughton.* Carroll and Duckworth then walked to Iffley, and sent transport back for the women and girls.

Alice's own recollection of the day (mistakenly she recalled that they abandoned the boat at Iffley) suggests that it was not only the rain which put a dampener on this particular excursion: Carroll's sisters, she thought, were

> rather stout, and one might have expected that, with such a load in it, the boat would have been swamped. However, it was not the river that swamped us but the rain. It came on to pour so hard that we had to land at Iffley, and after trying to dry the Misses Dodgson at a fire, we drove home. This was a serious party, no stories nor singing: we were awed by the 'old ladies', for though they can only have been in their twenties, they appeared dreadfully old to us.[†]

The downpour of rain, occurring only a few weeks before the all-important trip to Godstow on 4 July, is commemorated in *Wonderland* by way of Alice's tears, which are so copious that several 'curious creatures' start to flounder in the salty pool. Some of these animals are clearly identified: the Dodo (as an abbreviation of Dodgson) is Carroll, the Duck is Duckworth, and the Lory and Eaglet represent Lorina (Ina) and Edith. This episode also features, with greater adherence to the reality of that day, in *Under Ground*, which Carroll illustrated himself. Both his and Tenniel's depictions include a monkey or ape, at a time when Darwin's theories on evolution (following the publication of *On the Origin of Species* in 1859) were a matter of great debate. It would not be surprising for Tenniel to include such a topical visual reference, but for Carroll to do so, as an ordained clergyman, shows a degree of daring, albeit subtle. (It is likely that he attended a highly significant British

---

* Carroll makes no allusion to the school; it is the 1861 census which reveals that Mary Boughton (c1826–?), who was in fact unmarried, was the resident Sandford schoolteacher.
† *Cornhill Magazine*, July 1932, p7.

Association for the Advancement of Science debate on evolution, at which a famous verbal exchange occurred between the Bishop of Oxford, Samuel Wilberforce, and the eminent pro-Darwinian biologist Thomas Huxley. This was on 30 June 1860, at the brand new University Museum of Natural History, and an occasion when Carroll took many photographs of the important people in attendance.)

In the nineteenth century there was a productive paper mill at Sandford Lock, with an adjacent inn called (as it still is) The King's Arms. This was a popular spot for rowers, both casual and competitive, to stop off for refreshments, or to play skittles or quoits, and it features affectionately in a number of Oxford novels and memoirs.

33. Tenniel's animals (including the Duck, Lory and Eaglet), dry again after running the Caucus-race, watch as the Dodo presents Alice with her own thimble as a prize.

Just upstream of Sandford Lock is a large overflow weir, known locally as a 'lasher'. It has a mournful past, having claimed the lives of at least five Christ Church scholars. Among these were William Gaisford, the son of Thomas Gaisford (1779–1855), Henry Liddell's predecessor as Dean, who drowned here in June 1843, and Michael Llewellyn Davies in May 1921. He was the ward of J. M. Barrie, who composed Peter Pan (1904) for the entertainment of Michael and his brothers.*

∽ TEXTS ∽

('ALICE'S ADVENTURES UNDER GROUND')

In 'Down the Rabbit-hole', the first chapter of *Wonderland* and that of *Under Ground*, Alice has consumed the 'Eat Me' cake, and grown too large to get through the door to 'the loveliest garden you ever saw'. She starts to cry, 'shedding gallons of tears, until there was a large pool, about four inches deep, all round her, and reaching half way across the hall'. She shrinks when she fans herself until she is only three inches tall.

> **At this moment her foot slipped, and splash! She was up to her chin in salt water. Her first idea was that she had fallen into the sea: then she remembered that she was under ground, and she soon made out that it was the pool of tears that she had wept when she was nine feet high.**

Alice converses with a mouse, which has also slipped into the pool. It departs hurriedly when Alice mentions her cat, Dinah. Meanwhile:

---

* Barrie instigated the obelisk at the lasher: 'Michael Llewelyn Davies and Rupert Errol Victor Buxton, Commoners of Christ Church, were drowned here on 19th May 1921.' Another Christ Church death intimately connected with a classic children's book inspired by the Thames was that of Kenneth Grahame's son, Alastair, for whom *Wind in the Willows* (1908) had originally been written. He was fatally struck by a train in 1920, while a Christ Church undergraduate. Kenneth Grahame (1859–1932) himself had been at school in Oxford from 1868 to 1875, and both he and his son are buried in Oxford's Holywell cemetery, Kenneth having 'passed the river on the 6th of July 1932, leaving Childhood and Literature through him the more blest for all time'. The hatter Thomas Randall and his family are also buried at Holywell, as too, by pleasing coincidence, is Theophilus Carter – see Appendix 3 and *Alice's Oxford on Foot*.

> It was high time to go, for the pool was getting quite full of birds and animals that had fallen into it. There was a Duck and a Dodo, a Lory and an Eaglet, and several other curious creatures. Alice led the way and the whole party swam to the shore.
>
> They were indeed a curious looking party that assembled on the bank – the birds with draggled feathers, the animals with their fur clinging close to them – all dripping wet, cross, and uncomfortable.

In *Wonderland* this episode concludes with everyone getting dry by running the Caucus-race. Carroll's original manuscript, printed in facsimile in 1886 as *Alice's Adventures under Ground*, adheres much more closely to the reality of the day which inspired it. The Dodo (i.e. Carroll himself) says, 'I know of a house near here, where we could get the young lady and the rest of the party dried', and then

> The whole party moved along the river bank, (for the pool had by this time begun to flow out of the hall, and the edge of it was fringed with rushes and forget-me-nots,) in a slow procession, the Dodo leading the way. After a time the Dodo became impatient, and, leaving the Duck to bring up the rest of the party, moved on at a quicker pace with Alice, the Lory, and the Eaglet, and soon brought them to a little cottage, and there they sat snugly by the fire, wrapped in blankets, until the rest of the party had arrived, and they were all dry again.

When Alice again mentions her cat, Dinah, the birds make a rapid exit. She says to herself:

> I do wish some of them had stayed a little longer! and I was getting to be such friends with them – really, the Lory and I were almost like sisters! and so was that dear little Eaglet! And then the Duck and the Dodo! How nicely the Duck sang to us as we came along through the water: and if the Dodo hadn't known the way to that nice little cottage, I don't know when we should have got dry again.[*]

———————

[*] Robinson Duckworth had a fine singing voice (see pages 42 and 49).

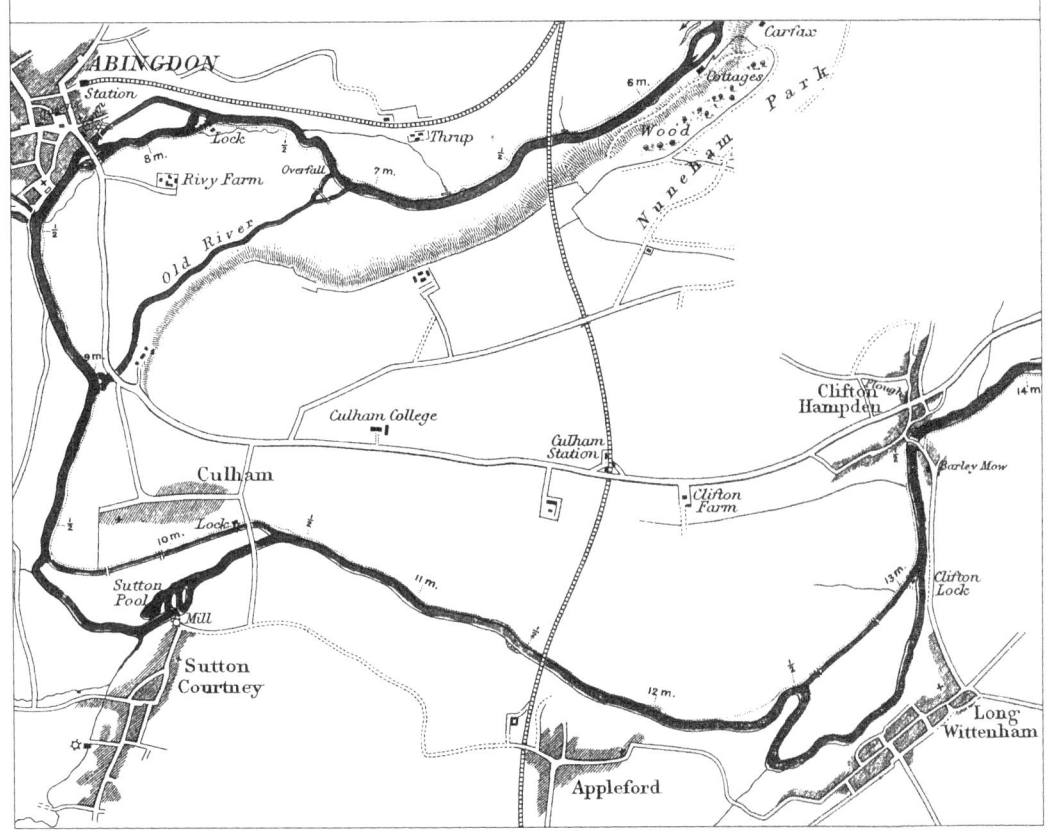

MAP 6

NUNEHAM TO CLIFTON HAMPDEN

Source: Henry Taunt's *New Map of the River Thames* (ed. 3) 1879, surveyed 1878.

34. A redrawn copy of a doodle by Henry Liddell (see Image 23). The original was auctioned by Sotheby's as part of a major 'Lewis Carroll's Alice' sale in 2001.

35. Tenniel's illustration from the chapter called 'Looking-Glass Insects'. On two of the boating expeditions to Nuneham in 1863 the return journey to Oxford was made by train. Other occasions when Carroll and the Liddells travelled together by rail include 5 July 1862 and 16 April 1863.

13

NUNEHAM

36. 'Nuneham Courteney' (sic) after William Tombleson, from *Tombleson's Thames* (1834). In reality the house occupies a much more elevated and distant position than the image implies, overlooking the landscaped parkland below. The area open to the public was downstream of this point.

7 MARCH 1855

Frank, Collyns, and I rowed to Nuneham, and called on Mr. Cooke,* who was from home.

1 JUNE 1862

Walked with Bayne to Nuneham and Clifton Hampden (a lovely village which I do not remember seeing before), returning by train.

24 APRIL 1863

Walked through Nuneham Park to Culham (2¼ hours) coming back by train.

9 JUNE 1863 (Tues.)

At 3 we (the children, Miss Prickett, and myself) set off down the river for Nuneham, reached it ten minutes past 5, walked through Nuneham Park to Clifton Hampden† (1½ hours) where we had a sort of a meal (bread and butter, and ginger-beer,) and thence to the Culham Station, and back to Oxford by the 7.47. Afterwards I went over and had tea with the three children in the schoolroom, leaving at half-past 9. A very pleasant day, to be marked with a white stone.

25 JUNE 1863 (Thurs.)

About 10 o'clock Alice and Edith came over to my rooms to fetch me over to arrange about an expedition to Nuneham. It ended in our going down at 3 a party of ten, the Dean and Mrs. Liddell and the Dean's father, the three children and Rhoda, Harcourt,

---

* Rev. Henry Pennant Cooke, who had just moved from Whitburn in Yorkshire to become the rector of Nuneham Courtenay.

† Jerome K. Jerome (*Three Men in a Boat*, 1889) was much taken with Clifton Hampden, and especially its inn, and caught something of the essence of Carroll when outlining The Barley Mow's 'story-book appearance' and its 'still more once-upon-a-timeyfied' interior.

Lord Newry and myself. We took a four-oar, and the last three
rowed all the way, the others taking it in turn to man the stroke-
oar. We had tea under the trees at Nuneham, after which the
rest drove home in the carriage (which met them in the park),
while Ina, Alice, Edith, and I (mirabile dictu!) walked down
to Abingdon-road station and so home by railway: a pleasant
expedition with a _very_ pleasant conclusion.

19 DEC. 1863

At 5 went over to the Deanery, where I staid till 8, making a sort
of dinner at their tea. The nominal object of my going was to play
croquêt, but it never came to that, music, talk, etc. occupying
the whole of a _very_ pleasant evening. The Dean was away: Mrs.
Liddell was with us part of the time. It is nearly six months
(June 25th) since I have seen anything of them, to speak of.
I mark this day with a white stone.

12 MAY 1864

During these last few days I have applied in vain for leave to take
the children on the river i.e. Alice, Edith, and Rhoda: but Mrs.
Liddell will not let _any_ come in the future – rather superfluous
caution.

27 MAY 1865

Went with Harcourt by river to Nuneham, taking the eldest three
Brodies.* We started about 2, and had tea at the house… We got
back just in time to witness the races from a little below Cherwell.
Lily rowed a little of the distance. A very pleasant afternoon.

---

* Margaret (1850–?), Ida (1852–1917), and Lily (1853–1916), the daughters of Benjamin Collins Brodie.

NUNEHAM

Nuneham, some six miles downstream from Oxford, was a favourite destination for picnic parties during the nineteenth century, thanks to the public-spirited attitude of the owners, the Harcourt family, with whom Carroll and the Liddells were on friendly terms. Their residence, Harcourt or Nuneham House, overlooked grounds which owed much to Lancelot 'Capability' Brown's genius for landscaping, and ran all the way down to the Thames.

Trips down the river to Nuneham feature in many works of Oxford fiction. Tom Brown's future wife visited during Commemoration Week, for instance, and Verdant Green accompanied his own future wife there a fictional decade or so later,

> when in a House-boat and in four-oars, they made ... a wine and water party ... to Nuneham, and, after safely passing through the perils of the pound-locks of Iffley and Sandford, arrived at the pretty thatched cottage, and picnicked in the round-house, and strolled through the nut plantations up to Carfax hill, to see the glorious view of Oxford, ... and paced over the little rustic bridge to the island.

Another author to fall under Nuneham's spell was the American Henry James, who incorporated 'the slanting woods of Nuneham – the sweetest, flattest, reediest, landscape that the heart need demand' – into his short story *A Passionate Pilgrim* (1875). En route from Oxford, where they hired a rowing boat near Christ Church Meadow (Salters' again, no doubt), the two protagonists 'encountered in hundreds the mighty lads of England, clad in white flannel and blue, immense, fair-haired, magnificent in their youth, lounging down the stream in their idle punts, in friendly couples or in solitude or pulling in straining crews and hoarsely exhorted from the bank'.*

---

* Repeated almost word for word from a letter that James wrote to his brother William from Oxford on 26 April 1869, in which he also alludes to the 'godlike strength' of the competitive rowers. (*Selected Letters* (1987) p29.)

Mr and Mrs Hall, in *The Book of the Thames* (1859), observed that 'the fine trees of Nuneham hang luxuriantly over the river – it is a perfect wealth of foliage piled on the rising banks' and: 'While Nature has been lavish of her bounties, Art has been employed everywhere to give them due effect. Open glades, solitary walks, graceful slopes, a spacious park, fruitful gardens – in short, all that can attract and charm in English scenery is here gathered.' The estate contained a large wood too, where cottages had been erected for the use of picnickers.

> These pretty and graceful cottages ... exist for the comfort and convenience of pleasure-seekers. Nuneham Courtenay has long been a famous resort of Oxford students and Oxford citizens; and seldom does a summer-day go by without a pleasant 'pic-nic' upon one of its slopes, amid its umbrageous woods, or within the graceful domicile, erected and furnished, literally, for 'public accommodation'.

Alice recalled in 1932:

> One of our favourite whole-day excursions was to row down to Nuneham and picnic in the woods there, in one of the huts specially provided by Mr. Harcourt for picknickers. On landing at Nuneham, our first duty was to choose the hut, and then to borrow plates, glasses, knives and forks from the cottages by the riverside. To us the hut might have been a Fairy King's palace, and the picnic a banquet in our honour. Sometimes we were told stories after luncheon that transported us into Fairyland. Sometimes we spent the afternoon wandering in the more material fairyland of the Nuneham woods until it was time to row back to Oxford in the long summer evening.

Occasionally, though, they found other means of returning home. An excursion to Nuneham on 25 June 1863 was a case in point. It was a day almost as significant as the inception day of 4 July 1862, because it turned out to be last time Carroll ever took the girls out on the river. But the day was remarkable for other reasons too.

Firstly, it was an altogether unprecedented ensemble: four Liddell sisters this time, as Rhoda, a week before her fourth birthday, came too, along with the Dean and Mrs Liddell, and his father, Henry

George Liddell (1788–1872). The rowing was undertaken by Carroll, Augustus Harcourt,* and Lord Newry,† making a total of ten, travelling in two boats.

On the journey down to Nuneham, it seems highly likely that the Great Volunteer Review would have been a main topic of conversation: most, if not all, of the party had watched it on Port Meadow the day before. The girls' games that day, as they went 'wandering in the more material fairyland of the Nuneham woods', might easily have had a military flavour. And as this is a wooded landscape that Carroll and the Liddell girls all knew well, it is not too fanciful to imagine Nuneham as the transposed setting for the different battle scenes in *Looking-Glass*, where Alice's encounters with Tweedledum and Tweedledee, the White King's soldiers, and the Red and White Knights are all set in or near woods. In fact, Nuneham hosted manoeuvres of this kind too, on occasions. Oxford resident Thomas Plowman referred to a 'sham-fight' here when he and William Harcourt (1827–1904), whose father owned the estate, were militia volunteers in the early 1860s.‡

The other unprecedented aspect of Thursday 25 June 1863 was that Carroll was permitted to travel back alone with the three older Liddell girls. A fortnight earlier, the four of them had also taken a train home (from Abingdon Road Station), again after boating down to Nuneham, but on that 'white stone' occasion Miss Prickett had been present too. This time, Carroll was their sole chaperon, a circumstance which he described as 'mirabile dictu!' – presumably on account of Ina's presence. She was now 14, and rather too old by the standards of Victorian convention to be unsupervised in the company of a man in his thirties (as Carroll himself had observed on 17 April that year).

One of the abiding mysteries of the relationship between Alice Liddell and Lewis Carroll is why, after this evidently highly satisfactory

---

* Augustus Harcourt (1834–1919) was the nephew of William Vernon Harcourt (1789–1871), then Lord of the Manor of Nuneham. As an inventive chemist he seems likely to have been, at least in part, a model for the White Knight.
† Francis Charles Needham (1842–1915), a Christ Church undergraduate at this time.
‡ Plowman, p149.

37. 'Cottages at Nuneham Courtenay' from Mr & Mrs S. C. Hall's *The Book of the Thames* (1859). The rustic cottage and bridge were built specifically to enhance the romantic scene, near the landing place for picnic parties.

day, the next page in Carroll's diary is missing, removed after his death, on the grounds presumably that the information there was thought too personal for publication.*

However, a scrap of paper discovered among the Dodgson family papers gives the gist of what the missing page contained. This note, in the handwriting of Violet Dodgson, one of Carroll's nieces, was headed 'Cut pages in Diary', and summarised the contents merely as: Lewis Carroll 'learns from Mrs Liddell that he is supposed to be using the children as a means of paying court to the governess. He is also supposed … to

---

* Carroll did not write a diary entry for every day. Friday 26 June was left blank, but the conclusion to the entry for Saturday 27 June is missing, and possibly the whole of Sunday and Monday too, as Carroll's next complete entry is for Tuesday 30th.

be courting Ina'.* In fact, the gossip about Carroll's supposed designs on Miss Prickett had been circulating since at least 1857 (see page 56), but rumours about Ina would have had far more serious implications. Probably by mutual consent, therefore – even if, indeed, there was any substance to this idea – Carroll agreed to keep his distance. No further outings were recorded with any of the Liddells, and even within the confines of Christ Church he remained deliberately 'aloof' for the rest of that year. There was one other encounter away from prying eyes, however, on 19 December 1863, and as Carroll marked this day with a 'white stone', the separation was presumably one he found hard to take. The next summer, even his offer to take the younger children out was turned down by Mrs Liddell, and the river's appeal seems to have diminished markedly for him as a result. Carroll's diary records only one further trip comparable to the many he had enjoyed in the company of the Liddells, when he took three of the Brodie children to Nuneham in May 1865.†

---

* Leach, p171.
† It reflects well on the Harcourts that the delights of Nuneham were open to all. The working-class children of Jericho enjoyed an annual boating treat here in the 1870s, for instance, at the instigation of Thomas and Martha Combe. 'The drum and fife band escorted them to Folly Bridge. At Sandford Lock, a pause for a bun and ginger beer! While on the lawn at Nuneham there was a good tea.' (Davies & Robinson, p36.) Almost certainly, the boat would have been provided by Salters'.

14

'THE END OF
MY MOVE'

Carroll must have been much affected by the abrupt end to the 'long dreamy summer afternoons of ancient times', as he described them in a letter to Alice of 21 December 1883.* Memories of this mysterious last day on which he took any of the Liddell girls out on the river must surely have coloured Carroll's writing of *Looking-Glass*. Certainly there is particular pathos towards the end, when the author's true self seems to emerge in the White Knight's words: 'I'll see you safe to the end of the wood – and then I must go back, you know. That's the end of my move.'†

It was too. The spoken Alicean stories which had had their printed genesis at Godstow, at the upper range of the river trips taken by Carroll and the Liddells, concluded at the downstream extremity of Nuneham. Carroll's imagination was not inhibited, but there were to be no more 'golden afternoons' on the river in the company of the Liddell sisters, no more 'voices and laughter like music over the water' with his favourite 'merry crew', and, sadly for the world of children's literature, no more opportunities for the impromptu creation of further 'news of fairy-land'.

---

* Collingwood, p230.
† In 1892, when Carroll presented a gift to an Oxford girl called Olive Butler, he signed it 'from the White Knight' ('Yours Very Sincerely', Grolier Club Exhibition Catalogue, New York, 1998, p84.)

Almost all of the subsequent encounters noted in Carroll's diaries were at the Deanery, including 'a very pleasant evening' with the girls and Mrs Liddell in December 1863, and give no hint of any particular animosity or suspicion. It was another seven years before his next meaningful, clearly totally unexpected, encounter with Alice, however. Carroll had already been gratified by an opportunity to photograph the children of the new University Chancellor, Robert Cecil, on 25 June 1870, when 'an almost equally wonderful thing' occurred: 'Mrs. Liddell brought Ina and Alice to be photographed ... first visiting my rooms then the studio.' This was the last photograph that he took of the Liddells; the last that he took of anyone at all came ten years later.

It seems clear that, without the company of the Liddell girls, rowing became much less of a pleasure for Carroll. He hinted as much to Alice herself, in a letter written on 1 March 1885, when asking her permission to reproduce the original manuscript of 'Alice's Adventures under Ground'. He addressed her formally, as Mrs Hargreaves, and observed that even if his contact seemed 'almost like a voice from the dead, after so many years of silence ... my mental picture is as vivid as ever of one who was, through so many years, my ideal child-friend'.* On meeting her husband again on 1 November 1888, after a gap of many years, he wrote in his diary: 'It was not easy to link in one's mind the new face with the olden memory – the stranger with the once-so-intimately known and loved "Alice", whom I shall always remember best as an entirely fascinating little 7 year-old maiden'.

When Dean Liddell retired at the end of 1890, Carroll – who was confined to his rooms on account of lumbago and synovitis of his left knee – was gratified by visits from the '4 ladies from the Deanery', namely Rhoda and Violet on 25 November 1890 and Mrs Liddell and Ina on 3 December, all of whom stayed for tea. Probably most gratifying of all, Alice – 'with whom my relations have never been what one would call "unfriendly"!' – visited him on 9 December, accompanied by Rhoda.

---

* Collingwood, p237.

There are slightly different endings to *Wonderland* and *Under Ground*. In both, Alice awakes on her sister's lap, when the cards fly up at her during the trial of the Knave of Hearts. In both versions the cards prove to be leaves, and both texts conclude with the thoughts of this older sister (therefore Ina). Of the two endings, that of *Under Ground* captures the 'Waterland' theme so aptly that I can see no better way to conclude than with the pleasing Oxford verisimilitude of Lewis Carroll himself. His penultimate paragraph relates how Alice's sister

> saw an ancient city, and a quiet river winding near it along the plain, and up the stream went slowly gliding a boat with a merry party of children on board – she could hear their voices and laughter like music over the water – and among them was another little Alice, who sat listening with bright eager eyes to a tale that was being told, and she listened for the words of the tale, and lo! it was the dream of her own little sister. So the boat wound slowly along, beneath the bright summer-day, with its merry crew and its music of voices and laughter, till it passed round one of the many turnings of the stream, and she saw it no more.

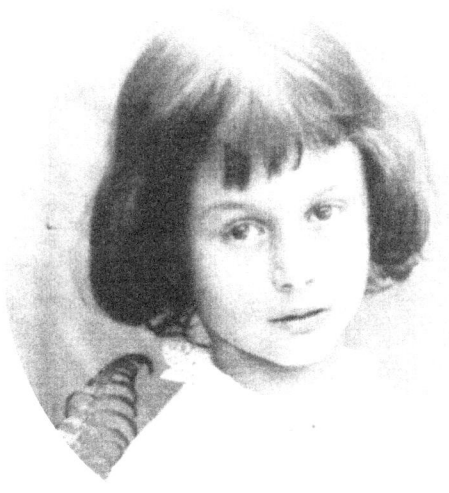

38. The photograph of Alice Liddell, aged eight, which Carroll had affixed at the end of the manuscript of 'Alice's Adventures under Ground' (over the sketch of her, shown on page 19).

PRICKETT FAMILIES OF BINSEY AND THAME

As outlined in the main text, there is a strong likelihood that it was Alice Liddell's governess, Mary Prickett (1832–1920), who influenced Lewis Carroll's creation of the Red Queen – 'the concentrated essence of all governesses' – in *Through the Looking-Glass*. Another common assumption has been that due to the long-established occurrence of the name Prickett in Binsey, Mary must have come from the village, and that this influenced Carroll's inclusion of the story of the treacle well at the Mad Tea-Party, based on the actual well in Binsey churchyard.

There is absolutely no evidence for this, nor is it certain that Carroll and Alice ever visited the well together – although it does seem likely, given that Christ Church held the manorial lordship of Binsey, and was patron of the church living (i.e. appointed and paid its curates, including Carroll's friend, Thomas Prout).

In reality, Mary Prickett's ancestors came from Thame, an Oxfordshire market town about 12 miles to the east of Oxford. Nonetheless, it is quite possible that some distant family tie did exist between the Pricketts of Binsey and those of Thame, and the short account which follows may prove helpful to further investigation.

Prickett of Binsey

There have been Pricketts in Binsey since at least the sixteenth century. The earliest reference in the archives of Christ Church is a document of 1598[*] in which Robert Pricket is named as one of four Binsey yeomen asserting their right to keep cattle on Port Meadow. The implication of this document,

---

[*] MS Estates 61/107.

maintaining that this right had been applied 'since time out of mind', is that Robert Pricket's ancestors had also lived in the village.

As farmers, the Pricketts continued to be associated with Binsey until the middle of the twentieth century. However, some early members of the Prickett family assumed a more distinctive role: that of the village publican. Records held at the Oxfordshire History Centre[*] show that the earliest identifiable licence for a Binsey alehouse was dated 3 August 1647. This was issued to Thomas Prickett, who remained licensed until 1661, followed by other members of the family – Alice, John, and another Thomas – until the early eighteenth century. Binsey was near one of the principal fords across the Thames into Oxford from the west, and its public house must therefore have benefitted from passing trade, both on land and on water. In earlier times, the proximity of the famous well of St Margaret seems certain to have engendered additional custom too, especially as the route through Binsey linked two other important religious communities: Godstow Nunnery to the north and the enormous abbey at Osney (until it was dismantled in the sixteenth century) to the south. There are accounts (almost certainly exaggerated, but presumed to have some basis in fact) that the neighbouring, now-vanished, village of Seacourt boasted in the medieval period some two dozen inns and lodging houses specifically to cater for visitors to the well.

The only tenuous connection to link the Pricketts of Binsey with those of Thame comes from the journal of Thomas Hearne (1678–1735), an Oxford antiquary and Bodleian librarian. Hearne visited Binsey on 22 December 1718, noting 'an old Well on the West Side of Binsey Church which they call St. Margaret's Well. They say it hath been very famous in the Popish Times'. On the same day he spoke to Thomas Prickett (c.1657–?), a yeoman farmer, who had been a church warden at Binsey for 38 years. He explained to Hearne the relevance of the streams which flow to the west of the hamlet: 'the Shire Lake because it parts Oxfordshire and Barkshire' (see Map 2), Wick Stream, the Dunge, and Sakworth. The Seacourt Stream, as the latter is now called, defines the city boundary to this day.[†]

---

[*] QSC/A5/1.
[†] For more on the waterways which define the ancient boundaries, or liberty, of Oxford, please see *What a Liberty!*, advertised at the end of this book.

Prickett of Thame

When the two men met again in 1728, Thomas Prickett told Hearne that as a member of the Militia he had provided military instruction at Thame School at the time of Monmouth's Rebellion (of 1685). Is it possible that Thame was a deliberate choice, on account of his having relatives in the town? The first appearance of the name Prickett in the records of St Mary's Church at Thame comes a few years later, when John Prickett, the son of John, was baptised on 19 December 1692. From him, the line to the Liddell family's governess, Mary, was as follows (all in Thame): Thomas, son of John, baptised 27 May 1703; Giles, son of Thomas, baptised 11 April 1734; Loder, son of Giles, baptised 22 February 1766.

The occupations of the earlier Pricketts of Thame are unknown, but Giles was an attorney, a profession also followed by his son, Loder, who married Martha Langford in Oxford in 1790. Their son James, Mary Prickett's father, was baptised at St Michael at the Northgate in Oxford on 27 January 1793. James married in 1826 Elizabeth Hitchings (daughter of Edward, who had been mayor of Oxford 1800/01 and 1811/12), and Mary was their third child, baptised at St Clement's in Oxford on 29 January 1832 (born on 3 January). At the time James described himself as a 'gentleman', living in Cowley Road.

By the time of the 1841 census, James Prickett was living with his wife and family of six children, aged between two and thirteen years, in one of the grand, newly built townhouses of Beaumont Street in central Oxford. It was not his own home, however, but that of his 85-year-old mother, Martha (née Langford), a woman of independent means. Any pretensions James himself had of being a self-sufficient 'gentleman' seem to have vanished, however, as he now identified himself as a 'college servant'. It was nonetheless an important role: butler at Trinity College for least some of the period between the 1830s and the 1860s. By 1861 the family was living in the very much more modest surroundings of Floyd's Row, a few minutes' walk from Christ Church – albeit still with one live-in servant. (Mary was in Llandudno at the time of the census (7/8 April), one of five staff that the Liddells took with them on an Easter family holiday.)

Mary Prickett was presumably engaged by Mrs Liddell very soon after the decision was made to move to Oxford in 1855, but is not mentioned in Carroll's diaries until 3 November 1856. She left their service to marry, at the age of 39, a wealthy wine merchant and widower called Charles Foster

39. (left) Miss Prickett, a photograph of unknown date and origin (*courtesy of Hodder & Stoughton*).
40. (right) Tenniel's Red Queen and Alice in 'The Garden of Live Flowers'.

(1809–1888). The ceremony was held at St Aldate's Church, immediately opposite Christ Church, on 22 March 1871. Her father, somewhat presumptuously, persisted in describing himself as a 'gentleman'.

This was not the first Foster–Prickett union. In an intriguing cross-generational alliance, Mary's younger sister Elizabeth (1837–1914) was already married to Charles Foster's son, John (1838–1873).* Then in 1873 their brother Frederick Prickett (1842–?) married Charles Foster's daughter Anne (1841–?)! On the death of her husband that same year, Elizabeth Foster (née Prickett) married Samuel Patey Spiers (1840–1891), son of Richard James Spiers (1806–1877), for whose diary see the footnote on page 115. Once married, Charles and Mary Foster took over one of Oxford's most prestigious coaching inns, The Mitre, in the High Street. It was to be Mary's home for the rest of her life. Caryl Hargreaves remembered:

> On one occasion when Oxford was very full, my grandfather [Henry Liddell] persuaded Mrs. Foster to turn out of her own rooms in the hotel in order to provide accommodation for Lord Rosebery. The latter, who knew all the

---

* A witness at the wedding in 1864, in addition to Mary, was Thomas Randall: by no means the only time that the putative Hatter and Red Queen met socially, as Spiers' diary reveals.

Liddell family well, said to the Dean that he was surprised to find the rooms of the proprietress of the Mitre Hotel full of photographs of the Liddells, and wondered how she had got them![*]

Surviving her husband by more than 30 years, Mary Foster continued to run The Mitre (residing there with her sister, brother-in-law, and numerous nephews and nieces) until her death in 1920. Apart from one other very early possibility, this tenancy of almost half a century is longer than any other known in The Mitre's 800-year history, as listed in *Round About 'The Mitre' at Oxford* (edition 2, 1929) by R. A. H. Spiers (Mary's nephew).

In summary, it would therefore appear that there is no direct connection between Mary Prickett and Binsey – even though it is tempting to discern a possible tenuous ancestral pattern between those early Binsey publicans and her later occupation. Indeed, her father had also been a 'wine merchant' in the early years of his marriage, and wine must surely have been within the remit of a college butler. It is not impossible that there was some connection. A hundred years later the Rev. Arnold Mallinson was in no doubt. In a St Frideswide's parish newsletter of February 1967 he stated confidently that Mary Prickett had been the great-aunt of Miss Althea Prickett (1880–1973), the last of who-knows-how-many generations of the family to reside in the village.[†] The facts do not bear this out, however (nor in respect of his assertion about the Liddell Door in St Frideswide's Church – see page 138). Interested readers may like to read more about the Prickett family and about Binsey in general in *Binsey: Oxford's Holy Place* (see Further Reading).

----

[*] *Cornhill Magazine*, July 1932, p2.
[†] Arnold Mallinson, *Quinquagesimo Anno* (1974) p214.

'ALICE'S SHOP'

This appendix is based on an article first published with the sub-title 'Shopping Around for the (Woolly and Watery) Facts' in the Lewis Carroll Society's *Carrollian* (Nos. 35 & 36) of December 2021. More detailed references to sources can be found there.

Tenniel's Shop

The first published suggestion that No. 83 St Aldate's was the shop depicted by John Tenniel (1820–1914) in 'Wool and Water' appears to have been in 1925, when Robert Gunther (1869–1940), a Fellow of Magdalen College, wrote to *The Times*. He was commenting mainly on the removal of some of the old buildings on the eastern side of St Aldate's, in preparation for the creation of the Christ Church Memorial Gardens. He observed that as well as opening up 'a superb view of the Christ Church buildings … the pulling down of high houses over the way has let light into that "little dark shop" where Alice wanted "to look all round", … the only shop in St. Aldates that has retained its original small-paned windows and the counter as shown in the pictures' of Tenniel.*

Now, Gunther was a respected historian, who had just commenced his fourteen-volume *magnum opus* of *Early Science in Oxford*. The following year he would embark on establishing the University Museum of the History of Science in Broad Street.† He also lived at Folly Bridge, where St Aldate's crosses the Thames, so would have passed by the shop, and quite possibly patronised it, on numerous occasions. He was not, therefore, someone likely to get his facts wrong, though there is no way of knowing the evidence for his assertions.

---

* *The Times*, 18 February 1925, p15.
† On display at the Museum is Carroll's portable box of photographic chemicals.

41. The earliest known photograph of No. 83 St Aldate's, in Williams & Madan's *Handbook of the Literature of the Rev. C. L. Dodgson*, 1931 (*courtesy of Oxford University Press*).

Certainly, although there is no firm evidence that Tenniel himself ever visited the shop, it seems highly likely that he would have done so on those occasions when he came to Oxford to row on the Thames. This was something that he appears to have done on a near-annual basis in the company of his colleagues at *Punch*.* Although the earliest of these excursions which can be dated came in 1865, it seems certain that there had been many before that, since it was rowing which facilitated a particular long-standing bond between Tenniel, who had first contributed to *Punch* in 1850, and a principal writer, Henry Silver (1828–1910), who did so in 1857. When departing from Oxford, the starting point was always the same as that used by Lewis Carroll: Folly Bridge, at the bottom of St Aldate's.

On 29 July 1865 George du Maurier (1834–1896) was one of the *Punch* party. Afterwards he wrote to his mother of meeting 'Tenniel, young Charles Dickens and 3 others to row back to Windsor; one of the most splendid holidays I ever recollect ... 70 miles; ce n'est pas mal.'† The '3 others' were Henry Silver, Fred Evans junior (whose father was the publisher of *Punch*, and also of Charles Dickens' early works) and Evans' brother-in-law, Louis Lloyd (son of an early patron of Tenniel).‡

The next year Tenniel made another 'pull from Oxford',§ and evidence of a third of his Oxford outings comes from the pen of the man himself, in the form of an unpublished lyric, 'From Oxford to Henley'.¶ Although this must have occurred after the illustrations for *Looking-Glass* had been completed (because it was inspired by the operetta *Geneviève de Brabant* by Jacques Offenbach, first performed in London in November 1871), the start of the river journey described by Tenniel is nonetheless relevant, because it was probably habitual.** 'From Oxford to Henley' begins:

---

* *Punch Supplement*, 4 March 1914, p11, p14. This issue was devoted solely to Tenniel, who had died a few days earlier.
† *The Young George du Maurier* edited by Daphne du Maurier (1951) p262. George du Maurier was one of the 76 people to whom Carroll intended sending presentation copies of *Wonderland* at the end of 1864, even though the two men met for the first time only on 17 January 1868, when du Maurier (who was born in France) agreed to cast his eye over the French translation.
‡ *Punch Supplement*, 4 March 1914, p11.
§ Henry Silver's Diary, 19–21 August 1866 (British Library: MSS/Adds/88937/2/13).
¶ The original is at the Harry Ransom Humanities Research Center, University of Texas.
** It may well have occurred the following summer. Richard James Spiers (1806–1877), a prominent Oxford shopkeeper, noted in his diary that he escorted Tenniel and 'the Punch party' around Oxford on 12 and 13 July 1872.

When you're rowing down from O-o-Oxford
Take your boat at Salter's Yard
And if you're wise and wa-a-ry
You'll not begin by rowing hard.

Clearly, therefore, it is quite feasible for Tenniel to have called in at No. 83 to pick up supplies prior to departing from Folly Bridge on a possibly large number of occasions. He would not have needed to stay long to absorb the broad details of the interior, because of his unvarying technique: 'I never use models or Nature for the figure, drapery, or anything else, but I have a wonderful memory: a memory of *observation* – not for dates, but anything I see I remember.'*

Lewis Carroll himself once told Gertrude Thomson, who illustrated the cover of *The Nursery Alice:*

> Mr. Tenniel is the only artist who has drawn for me, who resolutely refused to use a model, and declared he no more needed one than I should need a multiplication-table to work a mathematical problem![†]

In other words, Tenniel would not have sketched the interior *in situ*, but back at his London studio, from memory. This would explain the discrepancy between the number of window panes shown in the illustrations and those in the actual window: see Image 41, the earliest known photograph of the building, taken in about 1931. This method of working equally allows for the possibility that Tenniel's envisioning of the inhabitants of Wonderland was influenced by some of Oxford's citizens, glanced in passing – including a certain hatter, perhaps, living close to Folly Bridge! (See Appendix 3.)

Carroll's Shop

So much for Tenniel, but what about Lewis Carroll? Given the Shop's proximity to Christ Church, he surely cannot fail to have frequented it on occasions, and if so must have become familiar with the shopkeepers because it was run by the same couple for at least 20 years, and possibly much longer. The census of 1851 (the year of Carroll's arrival in Oxford) shows John Millin (1797–1883) as a 'green grocer' at the right location (based

---

* M. H. Spielmann, *History of Punch* (1895) p463; Cosmo Monkhouse in Easter Number of the *Art Journal – The Art Annual* (1901) p28 (the issue which marked Tenniel's retirement from *Punch*).
† Collingwood, p199.

on its position in respect to Clark's Yard, which still exists). With him was his wife, Mary (1802–1889). The couple were at No. 83 St Aldate's in 1861 and 1871, when numbering was specific, resigning their tenancy only in 1876. Such a long tenure would surely have made the couple well-known to Christ Church scholars and staff, and as Mary is therefore the prime candidate for exhibiting characteristics attributable to the Sheep, it seems appropriate to provide a short summary of her life.

Born Mary Baker in the village of Nuneham Courtenay on 30 May 1802, she married Charles Cheer of Oxford at Nuneham in 1825. By the time of the 1841 census Charles ('male servant') and Mary were living a few doors away from John Millin, labourer, in St Aldate's. Charles died the following year, and John and the widowed Mary married in September of the year after that, at Oxford's St Paul's. They may therefore have begun their grocery business at No. 83 as early as 1843.

In 'Wool and Water' the only item that Alice is able to buy at the Shop is an egg, something which the real grocery shop run by the Millins seems certain to have sold, and also the tea shown in Tenniel's image. His view also shows toys and what could be sweets.

Alice's Shop

For a few years from the late 1880s the premises were tenanted by a carpenter called Elijah Heath, whose 21-year-old daughter, Alice, was named as the 'shopkeeper' (and who might just therefore have had some justification to call her shop 'Alice's'!). From the 1890s until just after the First World War the shop continued as a greengrocery, run by Mrs Ada Castle, and subsequently, from at least 1925 until 1952, by Miss Rosa Jane Parker, who began listing herself as a confectioner in *Kelly's Directories* from 1929 onwards. Sweets had clearly been available before this, however. In Robert Gunther's 1925 *Times* correspondence he wrote: 'The bottles with sweets are there, but trade in toys has gone a few doors down the street, the "AƎT" at 2s has become a brand of chocolate, and the dolls are replaced by bananas.'

Sweets continued to be sold by Miss Parker's successors too. In *To Teach the Senators Wisdom*, a post-World War Two novel by J. C. Masterman (the Provost of Worcester College, and later Vice-Chancellor of Oxford University), the following reference occurs in respect of 'the authentic sweet shop which Alice visited in *Through the Looking-glass*':

It seems to me that in that shop the Oxford of Lewis Carroll is still alive. Sweet ration or no sweet ration, I dare swear that the sweets in those glass bottles have not been changed since Tenniel drew them.*

The plot of *To Teach the Senators Wisdom* revolves around a group of Oxford dons trying to decide which of the city's many highlights they should show to some American visitors. One is reminded of an Oxford undergraduate tradition, that of negotiating the underground section of the Trill Mill Stream in a punt or canoe:

> I fancy, though I don't know for certain, that this particular drain or waterway is used by Carroll when Alice makes her journey with the sheep. I made the journey myself one summer afternoon with three other men, and it so happened that when we emerged in what was then the new Christ Church Memorial Garden some people were leaning over the stone balustrade and looking at the stream as it flowed lazily out of the ground. Their faces when our canoe emerged stick in my memory – you see, it happened to be the day of Encænia[†] and two of us were in morning coats and top-hats. I think that scene would have pleased Lewis Carroll; certainly we must have looked not unlike a Mad Hatter's water picnic.[‡]

'Alice's Shop'

Although, for reasons outlined in Chapter 7, the Trill Mill Stream is highly unlikely to have actually been Carroll's inspiration, Masterman's novel does provide one other telling piece of information: the apparent first coining of the name 'Alice's Shop', in a caption to a photograph. The term is seemingly Masterman's own shorthand, however, since no actual sign with this name is apparent. The following year, however, 'Alice's Shop' appeared in print officially for the first time, in an advertisement in *Kelly's Oxford Directory* placed by the new proprietors, Thames Valley Art Productions. An 'olde-world' signboard proclaiming 'Alice's Shop. 15th Century. (Lewis Carroll's Old Sheep Shop). Confectioner, Tobacconist, Newsagent' was affixed outside at about the same time.

---

* J. C. Masterman, *To Teach the Senators Wisdom* (1952) p127.
† The ceremonial conferring of degrees as part of Commemoration Week.
‡ The pioneer of these subterranean journeys seems to have been T. E. Lawrence, better known as 'Lawrence of Arabia', in about 1908. Another keen canoeist was Gerard Manley Hopkins (1844–89) who described this means of exploring Oxford's waterways as 'paradisiacal' and 'the summit of human happiness' (Robert Bernard Martin, *A Very Private Life*, 1991). Hopkins' 1879 poem 'Binsey Poplars' is a lament for some distinctive trees on the riverbank near the village which were felled for use on the railway.

In 1965 the entire frontage of the building was refurbished, having qualified for one of 29 repair grants awarded by the Ministry of Public Building and Works that year. This grant was on account of the building being part of the ancient Littlemore Hall, but it was its association with Lewis Carroll which attracted media interest: the *Guardian*, for instance, on 29 April 1965 headlined its account 'Alice's Shop awarded a repair grant'.

The popular idea that the real Alice Liddell frequented the shop was encouraged in the 1960s, and gained considerable credence, the *Oxford Illustrated Literary Guide* stating in 1981, albeit cautiously, that 'Alice Liddell is said to have bought sweets' there. At some point, 'sweets' were narrowed down to Alice's 'favourite barley sugar'.[*]

To conclude this short history of an Oxford institution (having omitted mention of one tragic incident) let me finish as I began, with the earliest statement, that by Robert Gunther in *The Times* of 18 February 1925. His warning about the increasing dominance of large retail outlets is a sentiment which still resonates a century later:

> It is but a tiny shop, where humble folk can live for a small rent and make an honest livelihood. More such are wanted. May the day be far distant when Oxford, wholly in the grasp of the multi-store keeper, cannot stimulate the imagination of her Lewis Carrolls, and their juvenile readers.

———————

[*] Batey, p20.

HATTER MATTER

The following is adapted from the comparable appendix in previous editions of *Alice in Waterland* and an article in the *Times Literary Supplement* of 13 May 2013. There a new candidate was identified as a possible inspiration for the Hatter: a well-known Oxford eccentric called Thomas Randall, who was pushed into contention by Alice Liddell herself, as explained below.

Charles Dodgson himself never acknowledged that any of his characters were based on real people. It was a line that he was obliged to take, of course, given the risk of causing offence within the relatively intimate Oxford social and academic circles in which he moved. Yet there is no doubt that he intended many of the characters and incidents to be recognisable to Alice and her sisters as harmless private jests, and the following should be read with this thought in mind.

I have chosen to omit another candidate mentioned in previous editions: Francis T. Cooper (1811–1862), though his unusual combination of vending both tea and hats does certainly give pause for thought.[*] It is also only fair to mention, in advance of my own musings on the possible inspirations for the Hatter, this passing observation by Dodgson's nephew, Stuart Dodgson Collingwood, in the context of his uncle's earliest days at Christ Church: that one of the half a dozen or so men in his regular dining hall 'mess' was 'one who still lives in "Alice in Wonderland" as the "Hatter".'[†] If correct, it renders all that follows slightly superfluous, albeit providing pertinent insights into the delicate commercial tightrope that Oxford tradesmen of the time were obliged to tread.

---

[*] Mark Davies, *Alice in Waterland* (ed. 2) (2012) p109/110. It was Francis Cooper's son Frank who made Oxford synonymous with marmalade, capitalising on his wife's recipe.

[†] Collingwood, p47. Not Philip Pusey, nor George Woodhouse, whom he names, but possibly Apsley Cherry or Charles Hampden. See *Lewis Carroll's Diaries* X. p400/401.

Theophilus Carter (1824–1904)

'All Oxford called him The Mad Hatter,' wrote Rev. W. Gordon Baillie in a letter to *The Times* of 19 March 1931. 'He would stand at the door of his furniture shop ... always with a top-hat at the back of his head, which, with a well-developed nose and a somewhat receding chin, made him an easy target for the caricaturist.'

Baillie was describing his recollection of Theophilus Carter, and the particular caricaturist whom he had in mind was Sir John Tenniel (1820–1914), illustrator of *Alice's Adventures in Wonderland* and *Through the Looking-Glass*. Baillie was one of three correspondents whose letters to *The Times* formed the initial evidence for a supposition which subsequently became accepted by many as fact: that Lewis Carroll encouraged Tenniel to model his memorable character on Carter as an act of petty revenge for some unspecified offence.

The idea is dubious on several counts. Such vindictiveness would be completely out-of-keeping with what we know of Carroll's nature; there is no evidence at all of any connection between him and Carter, nor between Carter and the real Alice; and why had it had taken six decades since the publication of *Looking-Glass* in 1872 for the idea to surface? Yet in the absence of any other candidate, and as no actual likeness of Carter was forthcoming, the decidedly retrospective opinion expressed in those letters to *The Times* became more and more ingrained.

However, a photograph of Carter *did* finally emerge, courtesy of Frideswide Curry (née Bates), whose mother was given it as a child (Image 42). Although it featured in the newsletter of Oxford's Holywell Cemetery[*] as long ago as 1992, it was properly published for the first time in 2013, to accompany my *Times Literary Supplement* article. It was subsequently included in *Alice's Oxford on Foot* (see the advertisement at the end of this book) in the following year. The similarity is certainly striking – yet that proves little, as explained below: in a King-of-Heartsish kind of way, the verdict rather preceded the evidence.

Theophilus Carter was baptised at St Aldate's Church, opposite Christ Church, the son of Harriet and Thomas Carter, who was a 'college servant'. By the time of the 1851 census, Theophilus, now married with three children,

------

[*] The burial place of both Theophilus Carter and Thomas Randall (and some of their relations).

42. The only known photograph (post-1895) of Theophilus Carter (1824–1904) by the Oxford photographer James Soame. As a schoolgirl in the 1920s, Oxford resident Joan Bates was given the photograph by W. Carter – identified by Joan as Theophilus Carter's nephew – and it was he, not Theophilus, who inscribed it "The Mad Hatter, with compliments". I first published the photo, by kind permission of Joan's daughter, Frideswide Curry, in 2013.

was living just off Oxford's High Street, and working as a 'porter/cabinet maker'. 1851 was the year of the Great Exhibition in London, and it was a report in *The Times* (7 March 1931) about the recollections of numerous people who had attended the Exhibition as children which inspired the subsequent correspondence.

In a Wonderland sort of way, the initial reason why Carter's name was mentioned at all appears to have had no basis in fact. The first of the three correspondents to *The Times*, Mr W. J. Ryland, initially (10 March 1931) made no allusion at all to the Hatter, but wrote merely to assert that it was Carter who had exhibited what *The Times* had referred to as an 'alarm clock bed which tipped up and threw the occupant out at the appointed hour'. An alarm clock bed was indeed displayed at the Exhibition – in fact two were – but Carter's name is not associated with either in the Exhibition's *Official Descriptive and Illustrated Catalogue* (the title page of which, coincidentally, earned John Tenniel his first important acclaim).*

---

* A similar device features in *Verdant Green*.

Further doubt derives from the memories of a lifelong Oxford resident, Thomas Plowman, who was taken to the Exhibition as a seven-year-old. The 'bed that turned people out if they did not get up in time' was one of the three things that he most wanted to see. Yet he makes no reference to it having had Oxford origins, even though his own father had been 'secretary of the Exhibition' for Oxfordshire and 'an exhibitor of one or two inventions' himself.* One of the two beds was exhibited by Robert Watson Savage, the other by Theodore Jones. Theodore? Theophilus? Did someone, at some point, perhaps get their Theos in a muddle?

Mr W. H. Greene pointed out (*The Times*, 13 March 1931) that Carter's still greater claim to fame was as 'the doubtless unconscious model for the Mad Hatter'. Following Baillie's contribution, the correspondence concluded (20 March 1931) with a second letter from Ryland. Although he had known Carter reasonably well, he had been unaware of the supposed Carrollian association, strangely enough, and had himself always considered Carter to be 'the living image of the late W. E. Gladstone, and, being well aware of the fact, was always careful to wear the high collar and black stock so often depicted in *Punch* cartoons'. The photograph of Carter seems to bear this out. Nonetheless, Ryland concluded that Tenniel's Hatter was Carter 'to the life'. So, on the face of it (so to speak!), these three opinions, albeit expressed so very retrospectively, seem fairly persuasive (notwithstanding the alarm clock bed), and the 'Theo Theory' has over time become accepted by many as fact.

For the rest of his working life (from at least 1861 until 1894) Carter lived and worked as an upholsterer/cabinet maker at 49 High Street, and occupied No. 48 in addition between 1875 and 1883.† It is therefore just feasible that Tenniel – who never used an actual model – might have memorised on one of his early visits to Oxford (see Appendix 2) the features of a distinctive, hat-wearing shopkeeper, often to be seen outside his prominently located premises. However, it seems far more likely that Carter's adoption of the persona was retrospective, and that as public recognition of Tenniel's

---

* Plowman, p8 & p12. Lewis Carroll also attended the Exhibition, saying 'the first impression produced on you when you get inside is bewilderment. It looks like a sort of fairyland.' (Letter to his sister Elizabeth, 5 July 1851.)

† The premises at No. 48, meanwhile, have a later connection with a truly iconic Oxford name. William Morris (1877–1963), prior to his great motor-car enterprises, repaired and manufactured cycles and motor bicycles here from 1896 to 1908.

characters became increasingly widespread, Carter decided to model himself on the character after others noted the similarity.

A far more plausible candidate – if indeed Tenniel was influenced by the features of any Oxford resident at all – is a rather more noteworthy proprietor of a still more prominent High Street shop and riverside house: 'Jolly Tom' Randall.

Thomas Randall (1805–1887)

The utterances of the fictional Alice are extremely well known; those of the real Alice Liddell (1852–1934) rather less so. One reason is that she only ever published two substantial recollections of her childhood days, in the *New York Times* of 1 May 1932 and *Cornhill Magazine* of July 1932, as related by her son Caryl (1887–1955). In the latter she mentioned that a 'special pleasure was to be allowed to take Rover out for a walk. Rover was a retriever belonging to a well-known Oxford tailor, called Randall.'[*] The man she was referring to was Thomas Randall and although he was indeed in business as a tailor and hosier he more commonly referred to himself in census returns and commercial listings as a hatter. In any comparison between Carter and Randall, this does therefore give him what might be termed a head-start! The Hatter does, after all, state at the trial of the Knave of Hearts that he has no hats of his own because 'I keep them to sell', and Tenniel's Hatter, with his label stating 'In this style 10s 6d', implies a seller of hats, like Randall, rather than simply a wearer of one, like Carter.[†]

Alice also specified where Randall lived: 'a house built on arches over the Isis, which he christened Grandpont' (see Image 20). The unpublished 1862 to 1866 diaries of Randall's daughter Eliza (1836–1916) confirm that Alice visited Grandpont House regularly throughout the fateful year of 1862, always with the family's governess, Mary Prickett (1832–1920), whom the Randalls knew as Polly. Usually Alice would be with her sisters (Eliza dubbed the three Liddell girls collectively as Mary's 'chicks'), and they would often go on walks to Hinksey or Iffley, or on outings farther afield. There are also mentions of watching the college boat races, for which Eliza's home was supremely well situated.

---

[*] *Cornhill Magazine*, July 1932, p4.
[†] Randall appears to have been sufficiently well known not to need to advertise often in *Jackson's Oxford Journal*. Another hatter, G. Margetts, did though, especially to highlight the availability of his 'half-guinea hat'.

Eliza Randall and Mary Prickett also met frequently for other reasons in the years before the former's marriage in December 1865 to the penniless but musically brilliant former Christ Church scholar, John Stainer (1840–1901).* Ice-skating on the frozen Thames and boating are mentioned, for instance, and in November 1862 Mary recuperated from jaundice at Grandpont House, being visited there by a concerned Mrs Liddell. Occasionally, Christ Church confidences would be shared: 'Polly Prickett came home and account of Mr. Dodgson at Cheltenham', for instance, in April 1863 (when Carroll had spent several days in the company of the whole Liddell family at the Dean's parents' home near Cheltenham).

43. Alderman Thomas Randall (1805–1887), post-1861.

The three-storey Georgian mansion of Grandpont House still stands over a side-stream of the Thames near Folly Bridge, where the many rowing outings which were fundamental to Carroll's creation of Alice's adventures commenced. It is mentioned in the comic novel of 1850s' undergraduate life, *The Adventures of Mr. Verdant Green*, as too, in favourable terms, is Randall's High Street shop. It is one of many indications of the high regard with which Randall was held by both Town and Gown, the latter despite his prominent role in championing Oxford tradesmen in a high-profile and personally risky dispute with the University in 1847.

Many are the accounts, both in memoirs and fiction, of students running up enormous bills on tick with the tradesmen of Oxford, both parties being reasonably confident that public embarrassment would eventually be avoided, if it came to it, by parental intervention. This proved not to be the case for 22-year-old Worcester College student Edward Jennings, however, whose debts at the end of 1847 were assessed at an astonishing £2,213 13s 0½d, and his total assets as 'a silver Pencil case, valued at 3s'.† Randall,

---

* Stainer was the organist at Magdalen College at the time, and from 1872 to 1888 at St Paul's Cathedral, where he played at Alice's wedding, when she married Reginald Hargreaves in 1880. Alice was unable to attend Eliza's wedding as she had broken her leg the day before after a fall from a pony. (Eliza Stainer's diary 26 December 1865; *Jackson's Oxford Journal*, 6 January 1866.)

† *Oxford tradesmen versus the insolvent Jennings: a verbatim copy of the schedule of Edward Napleton Jennings: Discharged under the Insolvent Act, December 31st, 1847,* a pamphlet printed in Oxford, probably at Randall's instigation, in which the reports and correspondence from *The Times* were reprinted.

44. (left) Tenniel's Hatter and Dormouse at 'The Mad Tea-Party'.
45. (right) Thomas Randall, date unknown (*courtesy of David Pennant*).

describing himself as a hatter, was one of the 64 Oxford creditors who found little sympathy at the bankruptcy hearing in London, the commissioner deciding that it was not reasonable to expect an ingenuous young man to resist 'every species of credit proffered for every species of extravagance'. That extravagance included £195 for 'boats etc.' and £98 for *hats* (italicised by *The Times*). Randall himself was owed more than £70.

In its editorial of 1 January 1848 the newspaper encouraged its readers to 'heartily rejoice' at the verdict, believing that the 'trade harpies' of Oxford had got what they deserved. Randall, who attended the hearing in person, and was the only shopkeeper identified by name, was accused of having been particularly calculating in providing limitless credit at his 'ruination shop'. Asked why he had not thought to ask Jennings' college or parents about his creditworthiness, he replied that 'if he had done so, and the circumstance were mentioned, as it was sure to be, at a wine party, he might as well shut up shop'.

However, this danger of ostracism did not prevent Randall from writing to *The Times* (6 January 1848) with a 'feeble request to reply to your thundering philippic'. This phrase alone – especially clever as the name of the insolvency commissioner was Phillips – demonstrates the superior nature of Randall's education as a pupil of New College School. Indeed, in his memoirs, the Oxford don James Pycroft noted an additional service that surely none of Randall's peers in the retail trade could match: 'he was scholar enough to do verses and essays, as well as impositions, for the incapable and the idle'. It was an attribute corroborated by Carroll's colleague George Kitchin, who said that 'the great hosier of the High ... used to undertake, for a consideration, to compose the views of the haughty Undergraduate' to present as their own work.[*]

Precarious though it might have been to take such a prominent role in defending the often-vilified Oxford 'shopocracy', the Jennings episode evidently did Randall no harm. When he was elected Mayor of Oxford in 1859, the University Vice-Chancellor made the inaugural speech, causing Randall's old teacher and New College don, George Cox, to write:

> How well he was fitted for the important position *I* was well aware; how admirably he discharged its duties the University as well as the City loudly expressed at a subsequent dinner, given in commemoration of his Mayoralty. *Discipuli palmæ sunt præmia vera magistri.*[†]

On the same theme, James Pycroft summed up Randall as the 'link between the town and the gown'. One example of this soothing of centuries-old frictions between the University and its hosts was his instigation of a scheme whereby college servants, who often found themselves redundant during the University's long summer vacation, could find work at seaside resorts.

Another pertinent demonstration of Randall's even-handedness is that it was he who salvaged the Oxford University boat which had been victorious against Cambridge in 1843. The boat was talismanic in that it was this race at Henley which had elevated rowing from a minor pastime to *the* pre-eminent University sport.[‡] Oxford had won against all the odds despite being a man down. 'One effect the seven-oar race had on our generation at Oxford: it made boating really popular, which it had not been till then,' wrote Thomas Hughes,[§] who himself took up rowing soon after, with instant success (much like the eponymous hero of his novel *Tom Brown at Oxford*). The Oxford boat used in the famous 1843 victory 'was moored as a trophy in Christchurch meadow at the point where Pactolus poured its foul stream into the Isis' (close to the starting point of Carroll's many boat excursions, therefore). It

---

[*] G. W. Kitchin, *Ruskin in Oxford* (1904) p13. Kitchin identified 'Cicero' Cook, 'the learned scout of Christ Church', as the provider of a similar service.

[†] G. V. Cox, *Recollections of Oxford* (ed. 2) (1870) p445.

[‡] It was 'the event which really popularised boating in Oxford; the College races were before that year a mere pleasant incident in a summer term'. (William Tuckwell, *Reminiscences of Oxford* (ed. 2) (1907) p113.)

[§] Thomas Hughes, *Memoir of a Brother* ((1873) p73.

46. A (slightly cropped) photograph (probably mid-1860s) including, as identified by John Stainer: in the middle row Sir James Morrish (grey hat), sometime Mayor of London, and Thomas Randall (black top hat); and at the back Mrs Elizabeth Randall in the centre and her daughter Eliza Cecil Randall (later Lady Stainer) to the right. The other people in the picture are thought to be from the Margetson family, who were close friends of the Randalls *(courtesy of David Pennant).*

remained until 1867, when, 'rotten and decayed, it was bought by jolly Tom Randall, mercer, alderman, scholar, its sound parts fashioned into a chair, and presented as the President's throne to the University barge'.* Randall, a Thames Commissioner, could probably see the boat from Grandpont House. He retained the stern and prow for himself, and had them converted into stylish bookcases.

Either he or his father had already ingratiated themselves with Oxford's oarsmen. In June 1837, Oxford's Queen's College won a race against the top college crew from Cambridge, and 'the triumphant crew were immediately hailed by the flag of victory, which Mr. Randall had brought from Oxford with a most confident anticipation of the actual result'. Randall had also provided 'the handsome dresses of the crew, and the handkerchiefs and rosettes worn by the Oxford men who were present at the match', and the

---

* William Tuckwell, *Reminiscences of Oxford* (ed. 2) (1907) p114.

flag he made was considered to be 'in the most tasteful style of neatness, and does Mr. Randall great credit as the designer of the decorations'.*

Thomas Randall also clearly shared Carroll's concern for children. His obituary in *Jackson's Oxford Journal* of 24 September 1887 noted that 'daily, the children of the parish owed much to his liberality and kindness of heart, and about a month ago the infants spent a happy day in his field and garden and were well regaled by him'.

In Theophilus Carter's case, it was clearly a case of life imitating art, as other people contrived to see a similarity once the books had become famous, and Carter encouraged the idea. But if it *was* Randall who was the real inspiration for the Hatter, the writer of his *Jackson's Oxford Journal* obituary was closer to the truth than he could possibly have guessed in saying that he 'has left a name behind him that will long be affectionately remembered not only in the homes of the rich, but in the cottage homes of the poor'.

The Hatter is probably the most recognisable and reproduced of all Tenniel's characters, after Alice herself. One reason is that Carroll bestowed on this special creation the distinction of appearing in both of the books (albeit as Hatta in *Looking-Glass*), along only with his companion the March Hare, otherwise Haigha.† Let me conclude with one final cryptic comment on the matter of the Hatter. In the weekly periodical *John Bull* (20 January 1866) its reviewer of *Alice's Adventures in Wonderland* (who was aware that the author was an Oxford mathematician) wrote:

> She meets ... a curious specimen of the human genus, a hungry and tea-drinking *hatter*, the intimate friend of a March hare. We do not know but there is a cunning covert allusion in this late character to the famous Oxford man in the moon, and the increased payment for his hats at the time of a city election.

Was this Thomas Randall? There is nothing to suggest such behaviour in any account of him, nor have I been able to locate any (not so) 'famous Oxford man in the moon', so you may draw your own conclusions, if, as Alice might have been tempted to query at some tea-party or other, sketch book at the ready, it is even possible to *draw* conclusions!

---

* *Oxford Herald* (quoted in W. E. Sherwood, *Oxford Rowing* (1900) p70).
† I cannot resist mentioning Haigha's 'Anglo-Saxon attitudes', a phrase used as the title of a 1956 novel about academic rivalry and fraud by my great-uncle and Merton College alumnus Sir Angus Wilson, in which the White King's pertinent words from *Looking-Glass* appear on a preliminary page.

OXFORD COLLEGE BARGES

During the 1860s and 1870s the status of competitive rowing within the University went from strength to strength, and the importance of the college barges – threefold in purpose: as changing and storage rooms, as viewing platforms, and as college status symbols – increased accordingly. The records of the various college boat clubs are often incomplete, but from Clare Sherriff's 2003 *The Oxford College Barges* (from which much of the following is derived) it would seem that some ten or twelve barges, including some which were rented from Salter Brothers, would have graced the bank of Christ Church Meadow during Alice's childhood.

The first of these grandiose vessels ever to be seen in Oxford was a former London livery company barge, used by the Merchant Taylors for ceremonial occasions. It was purchased by the Oxford University Boat Club in 1846,[*] three years after the influential Oxford–Cambridge race of 1843, which elevated the importance of rowing as a University sport (see Appendix 3). This first barge was passed on to University College in 1854, and replaced by a new, purpose-built vessel designed by E. G. Bruton. Bruton's is therefore the vessel referred to in Mr & Mrs S. C. Hall's 1859 *Book of the Thames* (see Image 48). At the time it appeared to them 'sombre in style', but within a year had been 'richly decorated with colour, and displaying the armorial bearings of all the colleges'.

The export of ceremonial vessels from London to Oxford continued with Oriel College's purchase before 1850 of what is believed to have been the Goldsmiths' Company barge. Exeter College (also referred to by the Halls) acquired the Stationers' barge in 1856, and purchased a second vessel from Salter Brothers in 1873. This is an early example of what would become a

---

[*] The vessel had been acquired from the Merchant Taylors by two London boatbuilders, Edward Wyld and William Noulton. Wyld was a member of a long-established London family of boatbuilders and watermen of that name, my own direct ancestors.

lucrative business for the firm, which already rented barges to Trinity College in 1866 and to Magdalen in 1872. Balliol purchased the Skinners' barge in 1859, and Queen's owned the former Lord Mayor of London's barge from about 1860. Other colleges – Brasenose, Christ Church, and Pembroke for certain – also possessed their own barges at this time, Pembroke sharing theirs with New, St John's, and Jesus colleges after 1877.

Today little trace of this unusual fleet remains. Many barges survived until the twentieth century, but in the late 1930s they began to be replaced by permanent boat houses a little farther downstream (see page 73), and most of the barges themselves were broken up or dispersed. However, the former barges of Queen's (1903 or 1908), Corpus Christi (1930), and St John's (1891) can still be seen in the Oxford area (at Medley, above Iffley, and above Sandford respectively). Until 2011 part of the barge built by Salters'

47. College barges line the bank of Christ Church Meadow, with Folly Bridge in the distance, in Henry Taunt's view (probably 1870s) from the towpath on the south bank of the Thames. Grandpont House can be seen on the far left. (*Oxfordshire History Centre*)

for Keble College in 1898 was displayed at the Museum of Oxford in St Aldate's. Reopened after refurbishment in 2022, the Museum no longer accommodates it, but various items of Liddell and Carrollian memorabilia can be seen there.

48. 'State Barges' from Mr & Mrs S. C. Hall's *The Book of the Thames* (1859). The two vessels shown are the former Stationers' Company barge, purchased by Exeter College in 1856, and the new University Boat Club barge, built in 1854.

THE DIARIES OF THOMAS VERE BAYNE (1829-1908)

Useful and Instructive Discoveries

I was not aware of the existence of the unpublished journals of Charles Lutwidge Dodgson's lifelong friend and Christ Church colleague, Thomas Vere Bayne, when composing the first two editions of this book. As much of their content is mundane – the weather, meals and walks, visits and meetings – that mattered little in one sense, but Bayne does also happily provide the occasional important insight. Two notable examples are: four limericks by Dodgson, which have never previously appeared in any book; and the initial clues to the reality of a long-held Alicean Oxford myth. The text which follows is a much modified version of my article in the *Times Literary Supplement* of 1 July 2022.

Charles Dodgson wrote his first limericks in 1845, aged thirteen. This was the year before Edward Lear popularised this form of humorous five-line verse in *A Book of Nonsense*, but long before the term 'limerick' had been coined for the format.* Young Dodgson's precocious compositions were included in 'Useful and Instructive Poetry',† the first of a series of family magazines that he produced, with illustrations, for the entertainment of his brothers and sisters over a period of ten years. Here are two examples:

> There was once a young man of Oporta
> Who daily grew shorter and shorter,
> The reason he said
> Was the hod on his head,
> Which was filled with the *heaviest* mortar.

---

* According to the *Oxford English Dictionary*, although the format had been in use since the eighteenth century, the term 'limerick' itself was adopted only in the late nineteenth.
† Published by Geoffrey Bles Ltd., London, in 1954.

His sister named Lucy O'Finner,
Grew constantly thinner and thinner,
The reason was plain,
She slept out in the rain,
And was never allowed any dinner.

Charles Dodgson had grown up as the oldest boy of eleven children in the rural isolation of Daresbury in Cheshire, where his father was the rector. Bayne, the son of the headmaster of nearby Warrington Grammar School, was one of his very few regular companions of a similar age. Bayne matriculated at Christ Church in 1848; Dodgson did likewise two years later.

Only five limerick verses are known to have been composed by Dodgson as an adult. One was slightly risqué, included much later in life in a letter to a young actress on holiday on the Isle of Man (saucily equated to 'I love man'),* but surprisingly the other four, 'written by C. L. D. in or about 1856', have remained unremarked until now, tucked away at the back of one of Bayne's journals. All four limericks are in Bayne's hand, and were presumably either discovered or remembered by him long after they were composed, because his journals cover the years 1886 to 1891 and 1895 to 1900. The rhymes are of especial poignancy in that they refer to identifiable Christ Church contemporaries, albeit the names were omitted in the original.†

1. There was a Greek Reader named [Stokes]
    Who indulged in the mildest of jokes:
    But they had not a bit
    Of the genuine wit,
    So he had to enforce them by pokes.

Edward Stokes (c.1823–1863) was a Christ Church don until 1860, but had little subsequent interaction with Dodgson.

2. There was a queer Censor named [Gordon]
    A gaunt, haggard, wild sort of raw Don.
    With the look of a monk
    Who has been very drunk,
    If he had but a sack cloth and cord on.

---

* Collingwood, p407.

† An outline of the four men's life and careers can be found in *Alumni Oxonienses* (1888), the alphabetical record of all members of Oxford University between 1715 and 1886.

Osborne Gordon (c.1814–1883) was a Christ Church don until 1861, then rector of Easthampstead, Berkshire. During his second year as an undergraduate, Dodgson wrote to tell his sister Elizabeth on 24 June 1852 that after a conversation with Gordon, who taught him Classics, he had concluded that '25 hours' hard work a day may get me through all I have to do, but I am not certain'. In 1864 Gordon was one of 21 intended recipients of presentation copies of the first edition of *Alice's Adventures in Wonderland*. Bayne was another.

> 3. There once was a Censor named [Marshall].
>   Whose success in explaining was partial;
>   For no man ever knew
>   What he thought false or true
>   So obscure in expression was [Marshall].

George Marshall (1817–97) was a Christ Church don until 1857. Dodgson seems to have remained on good terms with him, and there were occasional encounters until shortly before both men's deaths.

> 4. An unfortunate Tutor named [Prout]
>   Never knew what he lectured about;
>   When they said "What's that word"?
>   He seemed not to have heard,
>   But in Liddell and Scott looked it out.

This is the most pertinent of the four rhymes. 'Liddell and Scott' refers to the authoritative Greek–English Lexicon published by Alice's father, Henry George Liddell (1811–1898), and Robert Scott in 1843. Thomas Jones Prout (1823–1909) proved to be much more of a genuine friend than the other three lampooned individuals. His role in inspiring the character of the Dormouse and the concept of the treacle well is discussed in the main text, and the association of Binsey with Oxford's patron saint of St Frideswide leads to another important revelation lurking within Thomas Vere Bayne's otherwise largely routine journals: the first clue in a trail which disproves an old Alicean assumption.

In Binsey's sister church of St Frideswide, close to the River Thames at Osney in west Oxford, there is a finely carved, free-standing wooden door, depicting the saint in a rowing boat on the River Thames. The tradition has grown that this door was carved by Dodgson's muse, Alice Liddell (1852–1934). It was a neatly attractive idea, given the treacle well connection,

4. An unfortunate Tutor named — —
   Never knew what he lectured about;
   When they said "What's that word"?
   He seemed not to have heard,
   But in diddell and Scott looked it out.

The four previous were written by C. L. D. in
or about the year 1856.

49. The fourth, and most pertinent (and impertinent!), of the limericks at the back of Thomas Vere's Bayne's diary for 1889/91. (*Governing Body of Christ Church*)

5 Friday.
More bitter wind, no rain. Have to work in Archives, and
bring on Rheumatism.
6 Saturday.   Collections begin
Short walk with Dodgson. Bitter day. Great afternoon
tea at the Deanery, where are to be seen the panels
carved for a door in St. Frideswide's, East End of London,
by the two misses Liddell. Warner comes and sings
to me in the evening.

50. Extract from Thomas Vere Bayne's diary for 5 and 6 December 1890. (*Governing Body of Christ Church, Oxford*) Carroll's own diary entry for 6 December was: 'Took a walk (first time since my illness began on October 24) with Bayne.' He had identified his condition then as 'a combination of ague, cystitis and lumbago'.

that both churches have strong Christ Church associations, and that Alice
– with the benefit of instruction from one John Ruskin – clearly did have
considerable artistic talent. For many commentators (including, I confess,
myself) the correlation of these factors was just too good to ignore. Sadly it
turns out that they were actually just too good to be true! Nonetheless, the
reality is probably the next best thing: the door was, it turns out, carved by
Alice's younger sisters: Rhoda (1859–1949) and Violet (1864–1927).

It is Bayne's journal entry for 14 December 1886 which provides the
earliest clue. That day he inspected 'Rhoda Liddell's excellent wood carving,
a very handsome table, also a picture frame'. The former was of sufficient
quality for this ageing lifelong bachelor – the Oxford University prohibition
on marriage had been lifted only in 1877 – to joke with her that 'it would
almost reconcile me to matrimony if I had a chance of such a gift'!

Then on 6 December 1890, after a 'short walk with Dodgson', Bayne
enjoyed a 'great afternoon tea at the Deanery, where are to be seen the panels
carved for a door in St. Frideswide's, East End of London, by the two Misses
Liddell'. (Alice was no longer a 'Miss', it should be noted, and was at this
time living in Hampshire as Mrs Reginald Hargreaves.) This is the self-
same door which is now at St Frideswide's Church in Oxford, and its story
is an intriguing one.

In 1881 a Christ Church committee which included Dean Liddell
instigated the creation of a Mission Hall in the deprived London borough
of Poplar.* Before the end of the decade sufficient funds had been raised
to construct a new church, the foundation stone of which was laid on 6
July 1889, and the first service held a year later.† In May 1891, the Oxford
newspapers were reporting that Rhoda and Violet Liddell's 'carved oak door'
was complete, and that 'the lower panels are adapted from Italian designs
and the top represents St. Frideswide'.‡

A few weeks later, the Liddell sisters visited Poplar in person to observe
the installation of their handiwork, which was described as a sanctuary door.
Sisters with a non-genealogical bond were also to the fore that day, because a
foundation stone was laid for an adjacent new Mission House of the Clewer

---

* H. St John T. Evans, *The Parish of St. Frideswide of Oxford, Poplar: Our First Fifty Years – 1881–1931* (Leighton Buzzard, 1931) p10.
† Evans, p19.
‡ *Jackson's Oxford Journal*, 30 May 1891; *Oxford Times*, 30 May 1891.

Sisters (the inspiration for the TV series, 'Call the Midwife').[*] The latter building still exists in Lodore Street, but the church itself fared less well: it was severely damaged during the first onset of the Blitz in 1940, and later had to be completely demolished. The Liddell Door, as it should now be known, somehow survived unscathed, and in 1947 it was sent back to Oxford.[†]

The door's return to its place of origin was recorded retrospectively in the 'St Frideswide's and St Margaret's Magazine' of February 1967, in which the now clearly wishful assertion that 'Alice carved it' has misled many commentators ever since.[‡] The Red Queen once pronounced, 'When you've once said a thing, that fixes it, and you must take the consequences' because 'it's too late to correct it'. Well, in respect of the Liddell Door, here, contrariwise, is a correction to those 55 years of consequences!

------

* *Jackson's Oxford Journal*, 11 July 1891; *Oxford Times*, 11 July 1891.
† London Metropolitan Archives (DL/A/K/01/16/051): letter dated 29 October 1947.
‡ Arnold Mallinson, *Quinquagesimo Anno* (1974) p214/215. Even the eminent architectural historian Niklaus Pevsner was persuaded. (*The Buildings of England: Oxfordshire* (1974) p334.)

51. The panel of the door carved in 1890/91 by Rhoda and Violet Liddell for St Frideswide's Church in Poplar. It shows Oxford's patron saint of St Frideswide arriving at Binsey by boat, prior to the events which led to the miracle of the 'treacle well'. The door is now displayed in St Frideswide's Church, Osney. (*Mark Davies, 2020*)

SOURCES AND
FURTHER READING

BATEY, Mavis — *Alice's Adventures in Oxford*, Pitkin, London, 1980

'BEDE', 'Cuthbert' — *The Adventures of Mr. Verdant Green*, London, Parts 1–3, 1853–57

BOWMAN, Isa — *The Story of Lewis Carroll*, Dent, London, 1899

CARR, Lydia et al — *Binsey: Oxford's Holy Place*, Archaeopress, Oxford, 2014

CHURCH, Alfred J. — *Isis and Thamesis*, Seeley & Co, London, 1886

CLARK, Anne — *The Real Alice*, Michael Joseph, London, 1981

COHEN, Morton N. — *Lewis Carroll: a Biography*, Macmillan, London, 1995

COLLINGWOOD, Stuart Dodgson (ed.) — *The Life and Letters of Lewis Carroll*, T. Fisher Unwin, London, 1898

The Lewis Carroll Picture Book, T. Fisher Unwin, London, 1899

CURTHOYS, Judith — *The Stones of Christ Church*, Profile Books, London, 2017

DAVIES, Mark & ROBINSON, Catherine — *A Towpath Walk in Oxford*, Oxford Towpath Press (ed. 2) 2012

DAVIES, Mark — *Alice's Oxford on Foot*, Oxford Towpath Press (ed. 2 revised) 2022

ENGEN, Rodney — *Sir John Tenniel: Alice's White Knight*, Scolar Press, Aldershot, 1991

GARDNER, Martin — *The Annotated Alice: Definitive Edition*, Penguin, London, 2001

GORDON, Colin — *Beyond the Looking Glass*, Hodder & Stoughton, London, 1982

HALL, Mr. & Mrs. S. C. — *The Book of the Thames*, Arthur Hall, Virtue & Co, London, 1859 (first serialised in *The Art-Journal*, 1857–58); and Virtue, London (ed. 2) 1877

HARGREAVES, Caryl & Alice	'Alice's Recollections of Carrollian Days', *Cornhill Magazine*, July 1932
HIBBERT, C. & E. (eds.)	*Encyclopædia of Oxford*, Macmillan, London, 1988
HUDSON, Derek	*Lewis Carroll*, Constable, London, 1954
HUDSON, Giles	*Sarah Angelina Acland: first lady of colour photography*, Bodleian Library, Oxford, 2012
HUGHES, Thomas	*Tom Brown at Oxford*, Macmillan, London, 1861 (ed. 3 of 1914)
JEROME, Jerome K.	*Three Men in a Boat*, J. W. Arrowsmith, Bristol, 1889, (Oxford University Press, 1998)
LEACH, Karoline	*In the Shadow of the Dreamchild*, Peter Owen, London, 1999
LOVETT, Charlie	*Lewis Carroll's England*, Lewis Carroll Society, London, 1998
MORRIS, Frankie	*Artist of Wonderland*, Lutterworth, Cambridge, 2005
PLOWMAN Thomas F.	*In the Days of Victoria*, John Lane, London, 1918
RIMMER, Alfred	*Pleasant Spots Around Oxford*, Cassell, Potter, & Galpin, London, 1878
SHERRIFF, Clare	*The Oxford College Barges*, Unicorn, London, 2003
TAUNT, Henry	*A New Map of the River Thames*, Taunt, Oxford (ed. 2) 1873 and (ed. 3) 1879
HENRY L. Thompson	*Henry George Liddell*, John Murray, London, 1899
	Christ Church, Robinson, London, 1900
WAKELING, Edward (ed.)	*Lewis Carroll's Diaries* (January 1855–December 1897 in ten volumes), Lewis Carroll Society, 1993–2007
WILLIAMS, Sidney H. & MADAN, Falconer	*Handbook of the Literature of the Rev. C. L. Dodgson*, Oxford University Press, 1931
ZEEPVAT, Charlotte	*Queen Victoria's Youngest Son – the Untold History of Prince Leopold*, Sutton, Stroud, 2005

INDEX

References to Christ Church, Charles Dodgson/Lewis Carroll, Alice Liddell and her sisters Lorina (Ina) and Edith, and her parents have not been included, nor the River Thames (or Isis) or London. Locations are in or near Oxford unless otherwise stated.

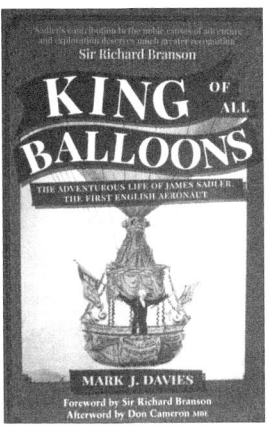